Gold Country's
LAST CHINATOWN

Gold Country's LAST CHINATOWN

MARYSVILLE, CALIFORNIA

LAWRENCE TOM & BRIAN TOM
CHINESE AMERICAN MUSEUM OF NORTHERN CALIFORNIA

THE
History
PRESS

Published by The History Press
Charleston, SC
www.historypress.com

Cover images: The Lotus Inn (*front top middle*) was one of the region's most renowned restaurants and watering holes. Area businessmen and politicians made deals there, and movie stars stopped in during duck hunting season. *Courtesy Bing Ong*; Moo Lung (Dancing Dragon), the first dragon in America (*front bottom*), came out of retirement in 1930 to parade on D Street, the main commercial street in Marysville, during the Bok Kai Festival. *Courtesy Bing Ong.*

First published 2020

Manufactured in the United States

ISBN 9781467143233

Library of Congress Control Number: 2019951267

Notice: The information in this book is true and complete to the best of our knowledge. It is offered without guarantee on the part of the authors or The History Press. The authors and The History Press disclaim all liability in connection with the use of this book.

This book is dedicated to the Chinese pioneers who settled in Marysville. They did not let injustice and other barriers stand in their path but believed in themselves and followed their dreams to attain a better life for their children, while also teaching them the importance of cultural preservation, identity and the meaning of family.

CONTENTS

ACKNOWLEDGEMENTS

Our first thanks go to Laurie Krill, our commissioning editor at The History Press. She was a past resident of Grass Valley, a town thirty miles east of Marysville, the subject of this book. She expressed a special interest in advocating for books in the surrounding area of Grass Valley. There were many requirements for this book that were different from the Images of America series, which we previously published under. She not only made the process easier but also provided invaluable direction and suggestions. This book would not have been published without her guidance and support.

The authors also owe a great debt of gratitude to the descendants of the pioneer Chinese families of the Marysville Chinatown. The first and second generations of the Chinese in America have all passed on, and much will be lost if information and materials are not documented and preserved. We organized a lot of photographs from private collections that were not used in our first book, *Marysville's Chinatown* (Arcadia Publishing). Some of those people we collected photographs from are no longer with us. That book was issued in 2008. Instead of leaving them unused, this book will preserve more of that history—after all, Marysville's Chinatown had such a rich history of the Chinese from the gold rush period.

Among the people who contributed photographs or assisted with this book are Sue Cejner-Meyers; Bertha Waugh Chan; Doreen Foo Croft; Paul Chace, PhD; Sherman Gee, PhD; Virginia Ong Gee; Wally Hagaman; Leonard Hom, PhD; Stanley Hom; Alisa Kim; the Honorable Frank Kim (ret.); Jack Kim, OD; Gene Sing Lim; May Tom Lum; Judy Mann; Bing Ong; Arthur Tom Jr.; Deborah J. Tom, MD; Gordon Tom; Mary Tom; Prentice Tom, MD; Mary Ong Tong; Ella Kim Wing; David Wing; and Brenda Lee Wong

The three libraries that contributed are the Sutter County Library, the California State Library History Section (CSLHS) in Sacramento and the Yuba County Library California Room. The files at the National Archives Pacific Region San Francisco were also a source of information.

INTRODUCTION

During the California Gold Rush, which started with the discovery of gold at Coloma, small towns started forming in the Gold Country. Due to the increasing number of Chinese coming to America starting in 1849, the Chinese began setting up shops in these towns. Because of their appearance, dress and mannerisms, they were viewed differently than the other miners. The Chinese stayed with themselves for support and survival. They established shops, boardinghouses, schools and temples.

These areas became Chinatowns. Marysville's Chinatown was one of the first established soon after the discovery of gold due to the large number of Chinese traveling through here on their way to the gold fields.

There were more than thirty Chinatowns established in California Gold Rush country. Of this number, Marysville's is the last surviving Chinatown in the area today. This one Chinatown provides a total spectrum of the Chinese in America—from the gold discovery period to the visits from Dr. Sun Yat-sen planning the overthrow of the Qing Dynasty to the celebration of the Bok Kai Festival.

For more than 150 years, the Marysville's Chinese community celebrated Yee Yuet Yee (second day of the second month on the lunar calendar). The Chinese refer to this as Bomb Day to signify the firing of bombs with the good luck rings. The name changed over the years to the Bok Kai Festival, due to a declining Chinese population in the Marysville area and the greater involvement of the total community.

As of today, Marysville still has two remaining Chinese organizations, Hop Sing Tong Association and the Marysville Chinese Community Inc. The Marysville chapter of Suey Sing Tong Association, established in the 1870s, was closed in 2015 due to a declining membership. However, the association building is still used once a year by the members from the other chapters of Suey Sing Tong Association during Bok Kai Festival to gather and worship at the Bok Kai Temple.

With the declining Chinese population, the Marysville Chinese community still feels that it is important to preserve the historical significances of their Chinese pioneers here. They feel that if Marysville's Chinatown was to disappear, the last link to the beginning of Chinese history in America would be lost forever.

Chapter 1

MARYSVILLE

THE BEGINNING

Prior to the discovery of gold at Coloma, California, in 1848, the location of the town of Marysville was the Cordua trading post and ranch for raising livestock. The trading post was located at what is now the southern end of D Street, the location of the present Chinese Bok Kai Temple, home of Bok Kai, the Chinese water god.

At the beginning of the gold rush, the location of Marysville became the ideal site for the beginning of a settlement, closer to the northeastern mines than the town of Sacramento. Marysville was described as the "Gateway to the Gold Fields."

The confluence of the Feather and Yuba Rivers provided the most expeditious method by river transportation to Marysville from San Francisco and Sacramento but also, later, for the shipment of gold to those cities. Once the gold rush started, the ranch became a point of debarkation for riverboats filled with miners on their way to the Gold Country east of Marysville.

Marysville's Chinatown started soon after the arrival of the first Chinese in 1849–50. Some Chinese, instead of proceeding to the mines, started establishing businesses in Marysville to equip those who were just traveling through to the mining camps to the east with mining implements and food products such as tea, rice, dried vegetables and salt-preserved items that were not available in the general marketplace. The first Chinese-owned businesses were established on First Street between A and B Streets.

In the beginning of the gold rush, there seemed to be no limit to what Marysville could accomplish. When California became a state in 1850,

Marysville was the ninth city to be incorporated in the state of California. There was talk of it even becoming the state capital for California. Developers began selling it as the "New York of the Pacific."

Marysville was the jumping-off point for miners to places such as North San Juan, Downieville, Grass Valley, Colfax and other mining towns to the east.

In the 1850s, roads in the California Central Valley were primitive and, in the wet weather, unpassable. In addition, crossing streams and rivers could be hazardous. River transportation played an important part in moving people, agricultural commodities and other goods around the region. To reach Marysville from San Francisco, river transportation was the quickest and easiest way.

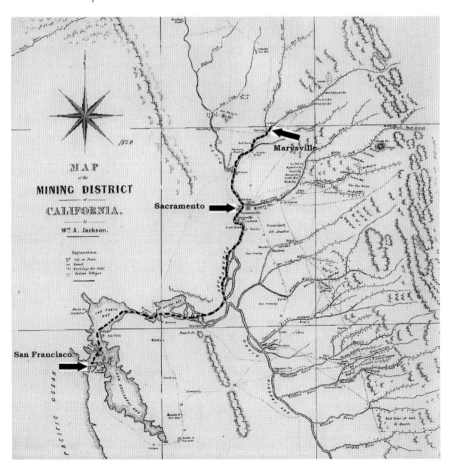

1850 *Mining District Map for Northern California*, showing the river route to Marysville and the locations of the mines east of Marysville. *Courtesy Library of Congress.*

Poster of the steamboat *Linda* in 1850. *Courtesy Yuba County Library.*

The *Linda* was the first steamboat to Marysville and Yuba City carrying passengers and supplies. *Linda* started operation in 1850, and eight months later, there were twenty-four sailing vessels at the landing in Marysville. Many steamers and sailing vessels were making regular trips from San Francisco to Marysville, as Marysville was the natural distributing point for the mining section in this part of the state.

By 1853, a regular line of steamers was leaving Marysville daily for San Francisco, with one steamer leaving at 7:00 a.m. and the other at 2:00 p.m.

With riverboat cargos being offloaded and repacked on mule trains, freight wagons and stagecoaches for the mines, the settlement at Marysville became a bustling trade center. The first newspaper published in Marysville was the *Marysville Herald*, with the first issue dated August 6, 1850. A post office was established in 1851.

When Marysville was first settled, the town consisted of canvas and wooden structures. Several fires devastated the town, and brick buildings replaced the canvas and wooden structures. Marysville became very largely a "city of bricks." By 1855, more than two hundred brick buildings had been constructed. There were several flourmills, an iron foundry, a woodworking mill, schools and a variety of small manufactories and craft establishments, including two daily newspapers.

With a population of almost ten thousand, Marysville was a thriving town by 1856. It was considered the second-largest city after San Francisco in California at this time.

The gold rush made Marysville a very wealthy community, and in 1857, more than $10 million in gold was shipped from banks in Marysville to the U.S. Mint in San Francisco. This is equivalent to about $300 million in 2019. In the following six months, another $4.3 million was shipped.

In an eighteen-year period, with the exception of six of those years, records by the State of California Division of Mines showed that Yuba County was the largest gold producing county in the state. Historians estimate that about 12 million ounces of gold were mined during the gold rush. That would be worth about $16 billion using 2019 prices.

The Yuba County Courthouse is the large three-story building in the center. The Sutter Buttes is not in the correct location but was added on the right to the picture. *Courtesy Yuba County Library.*

This is looking north on D Street from the down ramp of the D Street Bridge at First Street, circa the 1900s. *Courtesy Yuba County Library.*

Construction of the D Street Bridge, replacing the wooden structure. *Courtesy Gordon Tom.*

The main access from the south into Marysville was the D Street Bridge, so called because the bridge entry into Marysville was at the beginning of D Street. It was also known in the 1850s as the Yuba River Bridge. The original bridge was a wooden structure constructed in the latter part of the 1850s. Isaac McComas, a local contractor, listed in his job journal that on September 1, 1858, his company performed work on the tollhouse at the Yuba River Bridge. The 1885 Sanborn maps identified the bridge as a toll road.

There was a caretaker for the bridge, and the chief duty was to watch for possible fires on the bridge. There was also a gate at the entrance to the bridge that the caretaker would close to stop teams of runaway horses if they approached the bridge.

The permanent construction for the bridge started in the late 1800s, and with the completion of the D Street Bridge, it provided a more formal entry into Marysville. The bridge later became part of the state highway system in 1926 as US Route 99E, also known as the "Golden State Highway" and "the Main Street of California." It ran from the Oregon border in the north to the Mexican border in the south and connected all the major towns and cities in California's Central Valley.

D Street in Marysville became a very busy shopping district for the surrounding area. It was the main commercial street in Marysville, with most of the major retailers located there. At the northwest corner of Second and D

Members of the Joe Bong family and friends decided to have their picture taken on the D Street Bridge in 1920s. *Courtesy Brenda Lee Wong.*

The entry to Chinatown is the first street to the left after crossing the D Street Bridge. *Courtesy Gordon Tom.*

Streets was the famous Western Hotel, with a cupola on top of the building. In 1911, the hotel was home to the first elevator, steam heaters and electricity between Sacramento and Portland. It was rated as a five-star hotel. After ninety-five years, it was demolished in 1977.

The Feather and Yuba Rivers made possible the growth of Marysville during the gold rush period. However, the two rivers also became the major obstacle *to* growth because of their flooding. Hydraulic mining east of Marysville on the Yuba River raised both the Yuba and Feather riverbeds, making the town susceptible to flooding. In hydraulic mining, the miners would blast gravel hillsides with high-pressure jets of water, and after the miners extracted the gold, the sediment or tailings were deposited on the banks of the Yuba River. Due to the steep slopes and narrow canyon of the Yuba River, it created a unique environment that washed most of the hydraulic mining debris downstream.

A study of hydraulic mining debris by the United States Geological Survey in 1917 on the Yuba River estimated the amount of debris washed down the Yuba at 680 million cubic yards. The debris in some cases raised the riverbed up to one hundred feet. This made it more difficult to navigate, and riverboats could no longer make the journey to Marysville. At one point, the riverbed was higher than the street level in Marysville.

To control flooding, Marysville built levees that eventually surrounded the town, and the town limits remained within that levee system.

The population of Marysville remained stagnant, with little change during California's growth period from the late 1800s to the mid-1900s because of the levee system that surrounded the town. The population has not increased much since the gold rush days.

In December 1955, during a continuous downpour of rain, the town of Marysville was completely surrounded by water from all directions. The water was between fifteen and twenty feet above the street level. During the high water, Marysville was evacuated. As the water was getting higher, there was a possible levee breach at the D Street Bridge—the location of the Bok Kai Temple, the home of Bok Kai, the Chinese god that controls water and flooding. Water was slowly lapping the top of the levee at that location, and panic was setting in among the workers sandbagging the levee.

There were concerns that a break was imminent, and some of the workers were started to flee from the site. A newspaper reporter near the Levee Commission Office on First Street overheard an encounter between two men, one in a hurry to head for city hall and the other, an elderly Chinese man, who didn't seem to be in any hurry at all. "You'd better find a high spot," the one in haste said to the elderly man. "The levee is going to go out in a matter of minutes." "Not so," said the elderly Chinese man. "Not with

The levee system that surrounded Marysville protected the town from flooding in 1955. *Courtesy Yuba County Library.*

Bok Kai here." And, of course, the man was right. The Marysville levee did not fail; probably within minutes of its last remaining strength, the water suddenly receded quickly.

There was a break in the levee at Shanghai Bend on the Yuba City side of the Feather River that relieved the pressure on the levees surrounding Marysville. Some believed that the Bok Kai, the Chinese water god, played a part in saving Marysville from being flooded.

Up to the first half of the twentieth century, Marysville had many stores and businesses of various types within one square mile, and the town was a powerful attraction for shoppers and businesspeople from the entire region. Marysville became known as "The Hub." It was the town for shopping and entertainment at that time. All the major retailers—such as Sears Roebuck & Company, Montgomery Ward Company, F.W. Woolworth Company, J.C. Penney Company and J.J. Newberry—were located on D Street (State Highway 99E) or E Street. For entertainment, there were three theaters, a roller skating rink, a bowling establishment and many taverns.

Because of the limited growth due to the levee system surrounding the town, Marysville was losing its appeal, and the major retailers slowly closed or eventually moved across the river to Yuba City. With the completion of the Interstate 5 highway to the west, Marysville lost all of its prominence as the Hub City in the area.

Chapter 2
MARYSVILLE'S CHINATOWN

Marysville's Chinatown was one of the first established in California's Gold Country and is the last surviving one today. It was one of the oldest in America and was ideally located, offering merchandising services to mining camps to the north and east. It was regularly supplied with goods and materials by riverboats via the Sacramento and Feather Rivers. It was also one of the few Chinatowns in Gold Country that was not subject to violence against the Chinese during the anti-Chinese movement.

During the gold rush, Marysville's Chinatown was a very important town for the Chinese. It was the gateway to the northeastern mines in California and also a supply point for the miners. The beginning of Marysville's Chinatown started in 1849–50, when the Chinese started arriving from China. After disembarking in San Francisco, they used the riverboats to head to Sacramento, and some continued to Marysville. The objective was to get as close to the northeastern mines as possible, as the road system that was available was difficult at best.

The Chinese called Marysville Sahm Fow in Chinese, or the "Third Port"—Sacramento being Yee Fow (the "Second Port"). Marysville had also been called May Lei Wont. This is the transliteration of Marysville in Chinese.

As the first Chinese arrived in Marysville, some of them, instead of proceeding to the mines, started establishing businesses to supply the Chinese who were just traveling through to the mines. However, the majority remained in town for only a short time before departing to try their luck in the gold fields east of Marysville.

One of the earliest records of a Chinese business in Marysville was A'hoy in 1851. He had a laundry on the eastern edge of lower Marysville, and it was reported in the *Marysville Herald*, the local newspaper, that a fire started at night at his laundry and burned half the business section down.

The Chinese in the early days of the gold rush were not familiar with Western products, so they mainly frequented Chinese businesses. Many of the Chinese did not understand the customs, religions or language of the new country, and they felt more comfortable interacting with their own countrymen.

Some felt that they were here for only a short time, so they didn't feel a need to assimilate with the general population. They kept to themselves and formed their own town within a town. This was the beginning of the Chinatown in Marysville. Here the Chinese could get the food and other products they were familiar with. They could speak the same language and shared dreams and hopes, the hardship and adventure. It created the illusion that Chinatown was really China.

Almost all of the Chinese who arrived during the gold rush came from a small area in the Guangdong Province in southern China. Most of them who settled in Marysville were from a four-county area referred to as Sze Yup, the Cantonese dialect spoken in those counties. It was estimated that eight of every ten Chinese who came to America during the gold rush were from the Sze Yup counties. Of those counties, four of the eight were from just one county, Toishan.

尾利允唐人埠

MARYSVILLE CHINATOWN

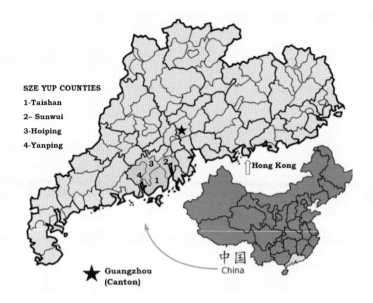

Map of Province of Guangdong in southern China and the counties where the Chinese immigrants came from. *Authors' collections.*

The Chinese from these counties would travel to Guangzhou (then known as Canton) and then to Hong Kong. During the gold rush period in California, Hong Kong had been a colony of the British empire since 1842, so it was easy for any Chinese who wanted to leave the country to obtain passage here on a foreign ship.

Since it took up to ninety days, depending on the weather conditions for sailing ships to cross the ocean to spread the word of gold discovery and up to another ninety days to return, only 325 Chinese arrived in 1849. In the next three years, the following numbers arrived:

- 1850: 450 Chinese
- 1851: 2,700 Chinese
- 1852: 20,000 Chinese

As the Chinese immigration to America continued, greater transportation capacity was necessary. In 1866, the Pacific Mall Steamship Company launched a new ship, the SS *Great Republic*, to accommodate the increase. It was the first of the ships built by Pacific Mail Steamship Company for the new line between San Francisco and China. It was a sidewheel steamship, the largest passenger liner on the U.S. West Coast and had capacity of 1,450 passengers.

The SS *Great Republic* being greeted by the Chinese as it sails into Hong Kong Harbor in 1867. *Courtesy Library of Congress.*

The *Great Republic* completed twenty-five voyages during its transpacific service from 1867 to 1877, transporting more than ten thousand Chinese to San Francisco, about 10 percent of Chinese immigration. As the Chinese started arriving in San Francisco, some continued on to Marysville. The first Chinese who stayed in Marysville settled on First Street between A Street and B Street. After their arrival, they carried over their customs, religion and traditions from China. They established shrines honoring a deity or many deities in homes, businesses and organizations.

In 1854, five years after the first group of Chinese arrived in California to work in the gold mines, the first Bok Kai Temple was built on the southeast corner of First and B Streets. This provided the Chinese community a formal place to meet their spiritual needs and to give thanks for safe travel, success in business and other ventures in the new land.

The 1855 Marysville directory of brick buildings listed only one Chinese merchant on the south side of First Street between C Street and Oak Street (formerly known as Maiden Lane). The directory also listed only two Chinese merchants on the west side of C Street between Front Street and First Street.

As the number of Chinese traveling through Marysville increased, the Chinatown started to expand with more businesses to provide products and services to support them. Marysville's Chinatown started to expand westward on First Street from A and B Street to C Street and later to D Street. It also moved north on C Street from Front Street, toward Third Street. In 1860, there were 227 Chinese in Marysville.

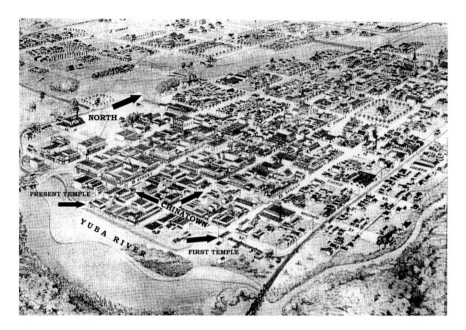

This 1871 illustration of the city of Marysville shows the location of the first and the current Bok Kai Temples and the expansion of Chinatown. *Courtesy Yuba County Library.*

By 1866, the first Bok Kai Temple at First and B Street had fallen into disrepair. A location for the second Bok Kai Temple was leased in 1869 at Front and D Streets next to the Yuba River, two blocks downstream from the first Bok Kai Temple.

Marysville's Chinatown was becoming a very lively community, especially on weekends and holidays. It was once second in size only to San Francisco's Chinatown. The Chinese population in 1870 for the largest cities in California were San Francisco at 11,728, Marysville at 1,417 and Sacramento at 1,371. The Chinese population was 30 percent of the total population of 4,738 in Marysville.

Marysville's Chinatown served as a major shopping center for those Chinese coming from the mines and outlying labor camps. In addition, it provided a place for worship and entertainment for rest and relaxation. On weekends and during holidays, the town drew in between five hundred to two thousand additional Chinese. Due to the large number of Chinese in the Marysville area, the *Marysville Daily Appeal* published an article in the March 28, 1867 edition:

CHINESE AND ENGLISH PHRASE BOOK
*We are indebted to Weil and Bernheim, booksellers in this city, for a copy
of the Chinese and English Phrase Book, with the Chinese pronunciation
indicated in English, which is specially adopted for the use of merchants,
travelers and families, by Benoni Lanetat. This publication is just the one
needed in every family, store or shop where Chinese are employed. Price $1.*

As the Chinese started arriving in America, it became clear that the environment was completely different from what they were accustomed to in China. Without guidance from family or village elders in a new land, the Chinese organized tongs—family, clan or district associations—for support and protection of its members.

These organizations played an important part in Marysville's Chinatown's history by helping its members adjust to life in a sometimes harsh environment. The organizations served as important meeting and networking places and helped those from the time they first arrived in America to settle disputes between members. They also hired attorneys to fight discriminatory laws passed by the national, state and local governments.

By the 1870s, Marysville's Chinatown had already established several tongs/associations, including the Suey Sing Tong, the Hop Sing Tong and the Gee Kong Tong (Chinese Masonic Lodge). The two tongs that were the most active and survived for the longest period were the Suey Sing Tong (until 2015) and the Hop Sing Tong, which is still active today.

In the past, disputes between the tongs that were not settled resulted in tong wars. The last tong war was between the Suey Sing Tong and the Hop Sing Tong in the early 1920s. The tongs are now mainly for socializing and carrying on the old traditions.

There were several opera houses in Marysville's Chinatown. The two most active were the Gee Kong Tong Opera House in the Chinese Masonic Lodge building at the corner of Elm and First Streets and the Low Yee Opera House on the west side of C Street between Front and First Streets. Both regularly scheduled top entertainers from San Francisco and China. Marysville's Chinatown had become the social, political and commercial center for all of the nearby Chinatowns.

During the early period of the gold rush, the Chinese were indispensable in the construction of the roads and railroads, the development of the irrigation system and agricultural farmland, the construction of the levee systems and other labor-intensive work. However, the 1870s saw the beginning of a nationwide depression in America. Because of the numbers of Chinese in California, they became the scapegoat. The rallying cry became "The Chinese must go!"

The Chinese were driven out of many small communities such as Chico, Red Bluff, Redding and Wheatland by killings and burning. Marysville's Chinatown welcomed its compatriots fleeing from these towns. Marysville's Chinatown became a place of refuge and was one of the few Chinatowns in California during period between 1870 and 1900 that did not have violence against the Chinese.

In 1878, the business directory of the Wells Fargo Bank listed two dozen Chinese businesses in Marysville. Even though there was a decreasing number of Chinese in Marysville, four years later, the number of Chinese businesses had almost doubled in number.

By the 1900s, the Chinese population continued to decline, and the Chinese population was down to 483, with a total population in Marysville of 3,497. Even with a decreasing Chinese population, Marysville's Chinese still played an important role in the establishment of the Republic of China. Dr. Sun Yat-sen, the first president of the Republic of China, came to Marysville twice in the early 1900s to plot the overthrow of the historic Manchu rulers in China and discuss the framework for a republican

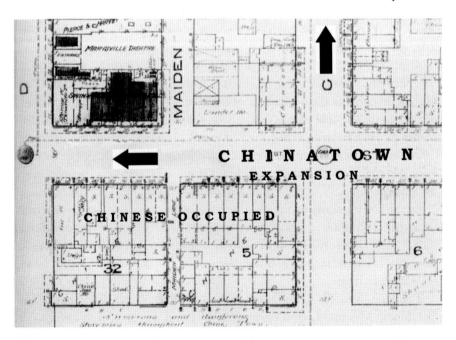

Marysville's Chinatown image showing that all the structures on the south side of First Street to D Street were now occupied by the Chinese. *Courtesy Yuba County Library.*

government. During his visits to Marysville, he stayed hidden between the Chinese Masonic Lodge building at 213 First Street and the Chinese Reform Party building at 306 First Street. The movement between the locations was to avoid being uncovered due to the concern that Manchu assassins would discover his location.

The center of Chinatown was at First and C Streets. Almost all of the Chinese businesses were on either First Street between A Street and D Street or on C Street between Front Street and Third Street. The 1913 International Chinese Business Directory listed forty-nine businesses and organizations in Marysville's Chinatown, the majority of them being listed as "General Merchandise" stores. Subsequent directories of Chinese businesses showed a gradual decline in the number of businesses and organizations in Chinatown.

Life on the blocks from First to Third Streets on C Street teemed with Chinese activities and businesses from the gold rush period to the 1940s. There were dry goods stores, markets, laundries and restaurants, all run by Chinese. The families operating these stores lived either upstairs or in the back of the businesses.

Starting in the late 1940s, the Chinatown families slowly began to move and settle in the areas of Marysville and Yuba City that were once unavailable to them. Adding to this movement, subsequent generations continued their education at a university or college and remained in the metropolitan areas since there were limited employment opportunities locally.

The 1952 Chinese Business Directory listed forty-three businesses and organizations. When Chinese businesses moved outside the Chinatown area into the main retail district in Marysville, they adopted English names, instead of the typical Chinese names, to draw on the broader market, leading to such names as Jay's Fabric Center, Jay's Women's Apparel, Savemor Department Store, Marysville's Furniture Store, Palace Meat Market, Park Grocery and Yuba Market. Not all of these were listed in the 1952 directory, possibly due to the English names.

By the 1960s, many of the buildings in Chinatown that were constructed from the 1850s were deteriorating, and many of them were razed in 1980s due to hazardous conditions or for redevelopment. Following are some of the buildings in Chinatown that were important in the lives of the Chinese here.

The Hong On Wo Company and the Gee Kong Tong (Chee Kung Tung or Chinese Masonic Lodge) opened in 1874 and was located at 211 and 213 First Street between Elm Street and B Street. When Dr. Sun Yat-sen secretly traveled to Marysville in his visits, this was one of the buildings where he

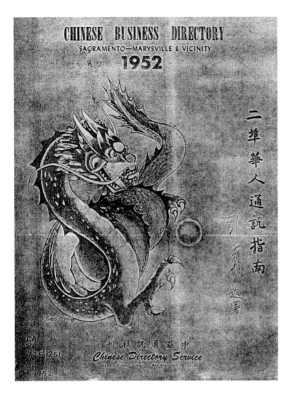

1952 Chinese business directory for Sacramento, Marysville and the vicinity. *Authors' collections.*

stayed. He seldom left the building since he and his colleagues were plotting the overthrow of the Manchu rulers in China.

The upstairs of the building was used as a community barbershop and a Chinese school before the school moved to 22 C Street. Many of the students were born between 1920 and the 1930s. The upstairs was also used as an opera house, with entertainers coming from San Francisco. This building no longer exists.

The second Chinese school was located at 22 C Street between 1935 and 1945. The wooden sign in the front with the Chinese characters noted that it was a Chinese school, and on the front window there was a sign noting that it was the Chinese Public School. There were twenty-five to thirty students in attendance. This building no longer exists.

The building at 226 First Street was constructed in 1888 and used as the third and last location of a Chinese school in Marysville from 1945 to 1970s. Prior to the school, it was the Chin Hang Lum Herb Company, owned by Tom Paul from the 1920s. This building exists with minor modifications. The interior was restored in 2018 and is presently the Chinese school museum, displaying Marysville Chinese memorabilia.

Above: 211–13 First Street. The Hong On Wo Company and the Gee Hong Tong. A Chinese school and opera house were upstairs. *Authors' collections.*

Right: 22 C Street. Chinese school, 1944. Sitting on the bench are Jimmy Yee, Frank Kim and Arthur Tom Jr. *Courtesy Gordon Tom.*

226 First Street. The last Chinese school in Marysville from 1945 to 1970. *Authors' collections.*

228 First Street. The Kim Wing Building. *Authors' collections.*

Number 228 First Street was constructed in 1858. Joe (Chow) Kim Wing opened a general merchandise store at this location in 1910. He was such a successful merchant of Chinese goods that he was able to add a second floor to the building in 1920. He named the structure the Kim Wing Building. The family lived on the second floor. He was well known in the whole Marysville community. Major modifications were made to the building in 2018, and it presently houses a spice shop.

The Kuomintang building was very important to the Marysville Chinese. It was the headquarters for the political party that ruled China from 1927 to 1949. All the Chinese in Marysville and in America at that time supported the Kuomintang political party. After the Kuomintang lost power in 1949, the building was converted to a youth center for Chinese children. Charlie Lim, born in Marysville's Chinatown in 1927, remembered the center during his teen years. "It was where we would get together because there was no place else for us to go. There was too much animosity against the Chinese in those days." The Kuomintang is presently the political party in power in Taiwan.

On August 10, 1910, the *Daily Appeal* reported on the opening of the store at 228 First Street by Kim Wing on Sunday. *Courtesy California State Library.*

部分允利尾駐黨民國國中

KUO MIN TANG
[CHINESE NATIONALIST PARTY]
230 FIRST STREET
MARYSVILLE, CAL., U.S.A.

230 First Street. The Kuomingtang Building. *Authors' collections.*

The building at 230 First Street was constructed in 1860. This building exists with no modification.

The Suey Sing Tong Association was one of the two major tongs in Marysville. It was active in Marysville for more than 145 years; however, due to declining membership, the Marysville chapter was closed in 2015 and merged with the Sacramento chapter. Although the Marysville chapter is no longer active, the Bok Kai Temple is still important to the members of

影撮會大表代次二十開部分头村美庄假部支西美縣黨民國國中日六廿月七年七卅國民華中

Members of the Kuomingtang party in July 1949 in front of 230 First Street, headquarters for the Marysville chapter of the organization. *Authors' collections.*

the organization. Once a year, during the Bok Kai Festival, members of the other Suey Sing Tong Association chapters journey to Marysville to worship at the temple.

The building that the Suey Sing Tong Association occupied is located at northwest corner of First and C Streets. It was constructed in 1862. Suey Sing Tong occupied the upstairs, with the address of 305 First Street, from the 1870s. In addition to a kitchen, dining hall and general meeting room upstairs, it included a gambling room. At various time, downstairs at 301 and 303 First Street was a general merchandise store and a tobacco store. Chin Yoke in the 1930s opened the Chong Wo store at the 303 First Street location.

The building had been rebuilt twice due to fire. The first time was in 1912 and was rebuilt quickly. The second time was in 1936. This fire gutted the complete building and destroyed all the precious tapestries and relics estimated at $25,000. This fire was reported on the front page of the *Appeal Democrat* on July 20, 1936.

The building was completely rebuilt and dedicated in 1937, hence that year being noted at the top of the building. The original plan for Suey Sing Tong Association Building was to cost $21,000, but the building underwent elaborate changes from the first specifications, bringing the total cost to well over $30,000.

The building at 232 First Street was constructed in 1858, and the second story was added in 1925. It was the Quong Hop Ket Kee drugs

Above: 301/303/305 First Street. Many chapters of the Suey Sing Tong Association came to worship at the temple during the 2018 Bok Kai Festival. *Authors' collections.*

Left: 232 First Street. The Chinese American Museum of Northern California. *Authors' collections.*

and merchandise store. In the 1930s, Lim Foo purchased the building and used it as a bean sprout plant, supplying bean sprouts to the many Chinese restaurants in town and the outlying communities such as Chico, Oroville, Colusa and as far as Dunsmuir, 180 miles to the north. Deliveries to distant locations were sent by rail.

Brian Tom purchased this building in 2005 and converted it to the Chinese American Museum of Northern California in 2006. The objective of the museum is to preserve and interpret the history of the Chinese in America. The museum had its grand opening in 2007. It was a huge success, with seminars by authors, professors and early residents of Marysville's Chinatown.

The Hop Sing Tong Association was established in Marysville in 1873 at 101½ C Street. The association moved into 113 C Street in 1918. In the 1950s, the association expanded its lodge hall to include the buildings to the immediate left and right, enlarging its facilities. During the Bok Kai Festival, the Hop Sing Tong Association has its annual meeting in Marysville for all the Hop Sing Tong Association chapters in America. Major modifications have been made to the building.

The buildings at 304 and 306 on First Street were constructed in 1853. 304 First Street was the Hong Wo-Sun Kee Company. The company was a major merchandise store that had offices in San Francisco. Next door at 306 First Street was the Chinese Reform Party office. This was one of the buildings where Dr. Sun Yat-sen secretly stayed during his visits to Marysville.

In the 1930s, the upstairs at 304½ was the home of the Lim/

113 C Street. The Hop Sing Tong Association Building before the remodeling and expansion in the 1950s. *Authors' collections.*

304/306 First Street. Hong Wo-Sun Kee Company and the Chinese Empire Reform Party. *Courtesy Yuba County Library.*

Chin family. Chin Yoke, the father of the family, owned the Chong Wo Store across the street at 303 First Street, located on the ground floor of the Suey Sing Tong Association building. The buildings at 304 and 306 no longer exist. The land is now part of a Chinese meditation garden.

Numbers 310, 312 and 314 First Street formed one of the original brick buildings constructed in 1853 in Marysville. It was the Tung Wo store and home for the Hom/Tom family for more than one hundred years. It had several major remodelings executed, the last to bring it up to earthquake standards in 1980s. This is the only building remaining on the south side of First Street between C and Oak (formerly known as Maiden Lane) Streets. This building still exists.

The King's Inn Restaurant at 101 C Street was one of two well-known Chinese restaurants. The building was constructed in 1856. This restaurant was owned by Ong Tall, a Chinatown community leader. In 1947, he opened the upscale restaurant Lotus Inn at 315 Second Street. The building still exists, with major modifications. As of 2019, it is an antiques store.

Above: 310/312/314 First Street. Home of the Hom/Tom families. *Courtesy Gordon Tom.*

Right: 101 C Street. Kings Inn Restaurant. *Courtesy Yuba County Library.*

103 First Street. Mama's Place or Hung Heung Low. *Courtesy Yuba County Library.*

Mama's Place Restaurant, or the Hung Heung Low Building at 103 C Street, was constructed in 1858. From the 1930s to the 1950s, it was the best-known Chinese restaurant in Marysville's Chinatown. The restaurant was owned by Harry Lim and his wife, "Mama." This building still exists with major modifications. To the left, at 105 C Street, was the dining room for Mama's Place. The dining room no longer exists and is now a courtyard for the Laughing Lotus Event Center at 103 C Street.

106 C Street. New Paris or Mee Wah. *Authors' collections.*

114 C Street. Marysville Hospital in 1907. *Courtesy Yuba County Library.*

New Paris, or the Mee Wah soda fountain and cigar store, was located at 106 C Street. The building was constructed in 1862 and is located on the first floor of the Suey Sing Tong Association building. From the 1930s to the 1950s, it was a front for a gambling establishment in the back room. The soda fountain with a counter and stools was in the front room and was frequented by many of the Chinese children. The gambling establishment was operated by Ong Tall.

The building at 114 C Street was used as the Marysville hospital. A new hospital was established at Fifth and E Streets in 1907, and this building was vacated. This building was later used as a home for the Chinese elders. The building no longer exists.

The Quong Fat Company was located at 124 C Street. It was connected in the back to the Shanghai Company at 306 Second Street. Both of these were fronts for a shared gambling room. After entering either from the C Street side or the Second Street side, it was necessary to enter through another door to reach a common gambling room in the back. The Shanghai Company was between the 49er Bar and the T and M Market on Second Street. The Shanghai Building no longer exists. The Quong Fat Company building still exists, and some minor modifications have been made to it.

Pago Pago, a popular upscale nightclub and restaurant with a tropical theme, opened in the 1940s. It had the largest dining area of all the restaurants

124 C Street. The Quong Fat Company Building. *Authors' collections.*

327 C Street. Pago Pago Restaurant and nightclub. *Courtesy Yuba County Library.*

315 Second Street. Lotus Inn, an upscale Chinese restaurant. *Courtesy Bing Ong.*

in Chinatown. Many parties given by the Chinese community were held here. It was located at 327 C Street at the northern edge of Chinatown. The building no longer exists.

The Lotus Inn was opened in 1947 by Ong Tall. It was an upscale Chinese restaurant at the northeast corner of Oak and Second Street. It was a very popular restaurant in Chinatown. In the redevelopment plans, the City of Marysville in 1976 purchased the Lotus Inn building and tore it down for a new library parking lot.

These were some of the buildings in Chinatown that were an important part of the lives of the Chinese families who lived there. The Chinatown now is not the Chinatown of yesteryear that comprised the homes and businesses of Chinese families. Gone is the ambiance of the Chinatown, with the aroma of stir-fried Chinese food from the many Chinese restaurants, the constant chattering in Chinese in the Sze Yup dialect heard from elders sitting on benches under the shade of a tree on the west side of C Street and the frolicking of the Chinese children playing on the sidewalks or in the playground area by the levee.

Today, Marysville's Chinatown is quiet, except for cars traveling through on First Street. Many of the old structures from the gold rush period were razed due to redevelopment or hazardous conditions. However, this is still Chinatown. It still has two Chinese restaurants, the Hop Sing Tong Association and the Suey Sing Tong Association Buildings, the Bok Kai Temple, the Marysville Chinese Community Inc. organization and two Chinese museums that are owned and managed by Chinese.

Chapter 3
THE BOK KAI TEMPLE (THE MUI)

The Bok Kai Temple is one of the key factors in keeping Marysville's Chinatown alive over the years, and it continues in that role today. It is the home of Bok Kai, the water god or the God of the Dark North. In past years, there have been many different spellings and transliterations of Bok Kai that have been used—Bok Ai, Bok Eye, Bok I, Buk Di, Peh-te and Pei Ti. For the historical references to the Marysville temple, it could be interpreted as "God of the North Shore," "God of the North Stream," "God of Water Virtue" and "Protector against Floods." These interpretations may have been adapted to this specific temple in Marysville.

However, the most common translation and meaning of the temple's name is North Stream Temple. It is the only known temple honoring Bok Kai as the central deity in America.

One of the most famous temples dedicated to Bok Kai, known by repute to all early Chinese immigrants in California, is the Ancestor Temple in Foshan near Guangzhou (Canton). It was built during the Northern Song Dynasty between 1078 and 1085 and rebuilt in 1372 as a Taoist temple at the beginning of the Ming Dynasty.

The Bok Kai Temple is also the only temple in the United States that still celebrates Yee Yuet Yee, as the Chinese called it. It is the second day of the second month on the lunar calendar, so it varies from year to year. It is also known as Bomb Day by the elder Chinese. The name Bomb Day derives from the firing of large firecrackers or bombs that launch good fortune rings into the air, with participants scrambling for them. It is a holiday honoring

This is the official seal for the Bok Kai Temple (the temple is called Mui in Chinese). *Authors' collections.*

Bok Kai, the water god. The date occurs somewhere in the latter part of February through the month of March. The celebration or festival is on the weekend following the official date.

Many of Marysville's Chinese were workers in the mines and on the railroads. They brought their traditions and religion with them, and after the Chinese started arriving in America in 1849, the first Bok Kai Temple in Marysville was constructed in 1854 at the southeastern corner of First and B Street. It was erected to provide for the spiritual needs of the community. It was constructed similar to the temples in China so that Chinese could give thanks and support for their journey to America and success in their fortune.

The property was purchased by the attorneys for the Chinese and later transferred in 1860 to the Hong Woo & Company. The Bok Kai Temple was operational for twelve years, from 1854 to 1866. It was said to be damaged by either fire or flood and fell into disrepair, no longer to be used after 1866. The City of Marysville later purchased the property from the Chinese to build a bigger and wider levee to protect against flooding from the Yuba River.

In March 1869, the Chinese community leased a brick building on Front Street and D Street for the present Bok Kai Temple. It was said that after the first temple was damaged, a prayer tablet from the temple was discovered at this location in the mud on the river side of the levee. The Chinese felt that this provided a sign that the new temple should be located here.

The building was one of the original brick buildings constructed in Marysville in 1852 facing Front Street and the Yuba River. The Chinese started remodeling the building for a temple soon after leasing the building and opened it for use in May 1869.

This temple is unique in that the Chinese in Marysville agreed to band together and build one temple that would be used by everyone. Other temples are built by a single association or organization and are often only open to those members. This temple has drawn countless numbers of worshipers and tourists from as far away as Hong Kong and Taiwan for more than a century.

The *Marysville Daily Appeal* from May 15, 1869, noted that the new Bok Kai Temple was to be opened to the public that day:

> THE NEW JOSE HOUSE
> *The Chinese Josh House recently constructed at the corner of D and Front street is now open to the public, and it is a perfect curiosity shop to all who never visited one of Confucius churches. We shall not attempt a description of the little fixings—they must be seen to be appreciated. The room is about fourteen feet square, and in the center and rear is seated an image representing a high dignitary, and at the right and left several less distinguished functionaries. A single wax taper was burning yesterday when we were present. In the evening, when the lanterns are lighted, it must look gay if not gaudy.*

Since 1869, the temple has been in continuous operation and is one of the oldest Taoist temples in California still serving the community with an official to assist in the religious services. During the Bok Kai Festival celebration, a large number of worshipers can be seen lined up to enter the temple to worship.

After eleven years in operation, in January 1880, major renovation and expansion started on the temple, expanding the Altar Hall and the surrounding structures from 60 feet wide and 20 feet deep to 75 feet wide and 40 feet deep. This added 1,900 square feet to the total structure. This included raising the central Altar Hall by 5 feet above the adjacent rooms and the surrounding ground level.

After the 1880 changes, the temple was repaired at various times, but the basic structure has remained unchanged. Insurance was purchased to cover any losses that might occur. The temple building was valued at $2,300 and the content within the building at $2,000.

In February 1880, two Chinese, Chow You and Yee Wat Chung, purchased the property and subsequently transferred the title of the property to a group referred to as the Trustees of the Bok Kai Temple. The trustees were the leaders of the four major Chinese associations in Marysville. This also marked the unification of the Chinese for a community spiritual center.

To maintain and keep the temple functioning, there were three sources of income. The most important source of income was the guardianship of the temple. Each year, this position would go to the highest bidder. This provided a safe income, and the more the guardian and the temple flourished, the more the guardian would gain monetarily through gratuities and sales of supplies for worshiping such as joss papers, candles, incense, paper money and so on.

In 1888, the highest bid was $354, and in 1891, the highest bid was $942. This was a period of time when the violence against the Chinese was increasing in other towns; Marysville was a place of refuge for them. The increase in the winning bid was most likely due to the increased usage by the refugees as a place to give blessing for their safe arrival in Marysville's Chinatown.

Another source of income for the temple was the sales of the bombs fired during the Bok Kai Festival; the third source of income was donations from businesses.

Bok Kai Temple in the early 1900s. *Courtesy Gordon Tom.*

The *Marysville Daily Appeal* on March 23, 1880, reported under the heading "THE HEATHEN TEMPLE":

> *The Boc Ky Church, or Chinese Temple recently erected on D and Front Streets, in this city, was dedicated on Sunday with much pomp, poise and enthusiasm. The management under the committee composed on Yeo Wood Gung; Wong Ting Oy, Chow You, and Lung Sing, was successful in all points, though the attendance was not as large as we anticipated. At no time during Sunday were there present over fifteen hundred Chinese. Main residents included. But they made noise enough for twice the number. At an early hour of the morning of the 21st instant.*

Clay roofing tile was added to the temple prior to 1950. The problems with adding the tile was that the structure was not reinforced to support the heavier load, causing damages to the support of the building. These were removed during restoration of the temple building in 2012.

Before entering the temple, over the doorway there is a decoration with mural paintings at the upper areas of the recessed porch entrance to the Altar Hall. The mural paintings were created by a single master artist at the time of the temple's dedication in 1880. This is a rare example of exterior decoration associated with Chinese religious architecture in the United States and in China.

Entry doors into the temple, with the mural painting above the doorway. *Authors' collections.*

The thirteen panels composing the mural painting have narrative scenes with figures engaged in different activities, calligraphy writing and decorative scenes of birds and flowers. The paintings of the temple are not only unique in North America, surviving more than a century, but are also among only a small number of surviving examples in the world. During the cultural revolution in China in the 1960s, many of the temple paintings in China were destroyed or painted over.

As you enter the temple, there is a raised threshold at the door meant to keep out evil. It was thought that evil spirits could transform themselves into human form with the exception of their feet, which remained hoof-like. In the early days, the threshold would require men and women to lift their gowns to step over it, revealing hooves instead of feet. The "non-humans" could be recognized or detected and barred from entering. It is also said that the raised door threshold prevented positive forces from leaving the temple and negative forces from entering.

After crossing the threshold, worshipers would beat a drum and sound a large gong near the door to awaken the gods to listen to their prayers. Incense was burned so the smell would please the gods and offered before they knelt to pray. The fragrance of incense permeated the surroundings.

Immediately behind the entry cabinet are several tables for the worshipers to place their food to be offered to the gods. There are several levels of food offerings provided at the table in front of the main altar. The basic offerings are fresh fruits; the most elaborate offerings could be a whole roasted pig, with the skin cooked to a golden mahogany color. Other food offerings include steamed chicken, barbecue pork and roast duck. Other common

The mural painting above the doorway to the temple. *Authors' collections.*

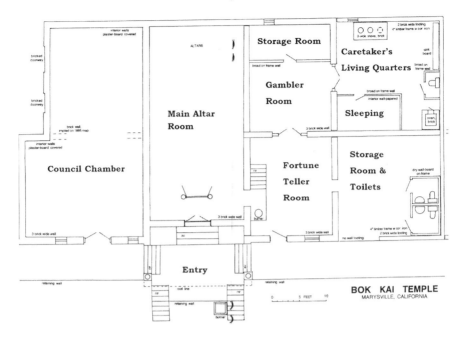

The floor plan of the Bok Kai Temple. *Courtesy Paul G. Chace, PhD.*

Bok Kai Temple entry. *Authors' collections.*

food items are eggs dyed in red, and steamed buns are sometimes added to the offering.

There is no formal seating. Each person worships in front of the main altar separately and not as a congregation, so seating is not necessary.

Several items are used in the temple by the worshipers, such as oracle sticks (Chinese fortune sticks) and divination blocks. Both are used for seeking guidance from the gods. Oracle sticks are thin, flat bamboo sticks with a number inscribed on the stick. The sticks are placed in a large canister, and the worshiper formulates a question. The canister is then shaken by the worshiper until one stick falls out. The number inscribed on that stick is matched to a numbered paper with the fortune. During Bok Kai Festival celebration, there are fortune tellers available to interpret the fortune.

Divination blocks are used in pairs and thrown to answer a yes or no question. They are made of wood or bamboo, curved on one side (the yin) and flat on the opposite side (the yang). Both are used while kneeling. When dropped, the future can be understood depending on their landing.

Offerings such as paper money or clothing were burned as a method of moving these items to the spiritual world. Directly behind the food offering is a long table with a jade tablet bearing inscriptions of deities, incense burners,

Whole roast pigs to be provided to the gods for worship. *Authors' collections*.

divination sticks, oracle books and other ceremonial objects. The jade tablet is also carried to the site to oversee the firing of the bomb rites on Sunday during Bok Kai Festival.

Immediately behind this table on the altar are the five main gods, with Bok Kai in the center flanked by two gods on each side. Facing the altar, on the left are Quan Ying, the Goddess of Mercy, and Quan Gung, the God of War and Peace. On the right are Yuk Fung, the Secretary of State God, and Sing Moo, the Goddess of Safe Travel. Behind each god on the altar is a mirror. Because evil spirits do not have a reflection, they could easily be recognized and ousted from the temple.

Jade tablet with names of gods and goddesses inscribed. *Authors' collections.*

On the back wall above Bok Kai is a painting of a black dragon with flames shooting from its mouth. The dragon is shown rising from a mist with glaring eyes facing the entry to the temple and the river. Since it was hidden by soot over the years, this painting was not visible and until recent restoration of the wall exposed it.

There is no documentation of the significances or the placement of the painting of the dragon in the temple, but in Chinese mythology, the dragon symbolizes potent and auspicious powers, particularly control over water, rainfall, typhoons and floods. It is also a symbol of power, strength and good luck for people who are worthy of it. Since the dragon is strongly associated with water and weather, it seems most appropriate to have it display with Bok Kai facing the Yuba River.

The temple has two wings to either side; both are about five feet lower than the elevated main altar room. To the left or the west wing is the Council Chamber, separated by a wood partition screen into two rooms of roughly equal size. The Council Chamber was used for formal temple meetings, a school and community functions. The present use is primarily for storage of the three hundred historical artifacts, including ceremonial and parade objects such as a sedan chair, banners and Moo Lung, the first parade dragon. This room is being developed into a museum to display the historical artifacts and provide a learning center for future generations.

To the right or the east wing, there are several rooms. The first room entering from either the altar room or from the outside is considered the

Black dragon on the back wall of the altar. *Authors' collections.*

The Council Chamber. *Courtesy Gordon Tom.*

Fortune Teller's room. From this room, connected by doorways, are the Gamblers' room, with a storage room to the left and another storage room and toilets straight ahead. The caretaker's living quarters is entered from the Gamblers' room.

The Bok Kai building has gone through many changes over the years. Because of the age of the building, much work was done in the 1960s and 1980s to maintain the structure's integrity. Further deterioration has occurred since that time.

In 1975, the Bok Kai Temple was added to the prestigious National Register of Historic Places (no. 75000498). It was made a California State Historical Landmark (no. 889) on October 18, 1976. A historical plaque was placed by the State Department of Parks and Recreation in cooperation with the Yuba County Historical Commission on that date:

> *Dedicated March 21, 1880, this building replaced the first temple built nearby in the early 1850s. It has been a Chinese community project since 1866, serving as a meeting hall, court, school, and place of worship. In this "Palace of Many Saints," Bok Eye, the water god, is the central deity and has been celebrated in Marysville on Bomb Day since Chinese settled here. California Historical Register Landmark No. 889*

Above: This is the Fortune Teller's room with the fortune teller's slips hanging on the board to the right. *Authors' collections.*

Left: This is the entry to the Gamblers' room, a storage room and the caretaker's living quarters. *Authors' collections.*

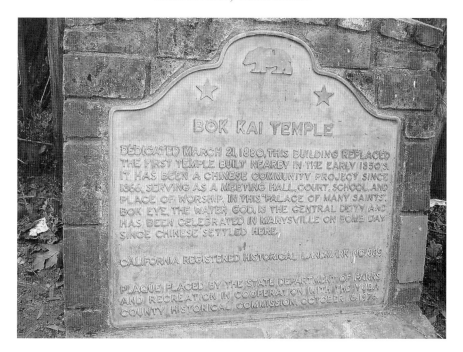

Plaque placed by the State Department of Parks and Recreation in cooperation of the Yuba County Historical Commission, October 16, 1976. *Authors' collections.*

When the D Street Bridge entering Marysville was realigned over to E Street, the D Street bridge ramp location was developed into a park. The Bok Kai portal and pavilion was conceived and constructed by the Marysville Kiwanis Club in 1978 at the park's location. This provided for a more formal entrance to the temple entry gate next to the levee.

The Two Foo Dogs (or Imperial Guardian Lions) at either side of the portal were a gift from Peikang, Marysville's Sister City in Taiwan, in the late 1970s. They provide protection for the temple and stop malicious intentions from entering.

In 2001, the temple was listed in the annual "America's 11 Most Endangered Places" list by the National Trust for Historical Preservation. This listing identifies places across America that are threatened by neglect, insufficient funds, inappropriate development or insensitive public policy.

Because of this concern, the City of Marysville and the Friends of the Marysville Bok Kai Temple organization retained the Architectural Resources Group (ARG) in 2002 to produce a Historic Structure Report on the temple. The report provided an assessment of the existing conditions and recommendations for correcting any deficiencies and for future stabilization

Portal and pavilion, constructed by the Marysville Kiwanis Club in 1978. *Authors' collections.*

in line with the State Historical Building Code, to ensure that any corrections of deficiencies don't adversely affect the significant historic resources of the temple. With a variety of fundraising events to correct the deficiencies, the temple was completely restored in 2012.

The Bok Kai Temple since 1869 has been and still is a very active temple year-round and is used extensively during the Bok Kai Festival celebration. It is a well-known temple, and people from not only the surrounding communities but also other states and foreign countries visit to honor the gods and seek guidance here.

Chapter 4

BOK KAI AND THE OTHER GODS

Chinese traditional religion is polytheistic, featuring the worship of or belief in multiple deities. There are more than two hundred gods and goddesses that are worshiped in China, not counting the numerous spirits. It was believed that the gods kept the universe functioning in harmony. Many of the Chinese gods were human once and, because of their good deeds and heavenly achievements, were elevated as gods.

Each village had a village temple where many gods were recognized and worshiped, with one major god that was the protector of that village. The Bok Kai Temple is an example of this with multiple gods worshiped in the temple, with Bok Kai the major god. This is the reason one of the temple's wooden plaques bears in Chinese writing, "Temple of Many Saints."

All of the gods and goddesses were important to the people of ancient China, but the "choice of Gods in the Temple," as quoted by Joe Lung Kim, a previous caretaker of the Bok Kai Temple, "seems to represent the spiritual wishes and the gratitude of the people who started the temple."

As you enter the present temple and walk around the display table, Bok Kai and four other gods are displayed on the main altar against the back wall. Each of these gods has its own special area of power and influence, but Bok Kai is the central deity in this place of worship and is situated in the center of the main altar, prominently spotlighted. He is flanked by the four other gods, two on each side.

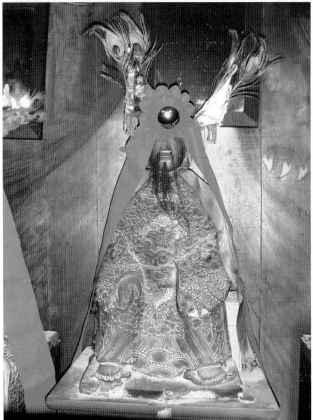

Above: Gods on the main altar in the temple. *Authors' collections.*

Left: Bok Kai, the God of the Dark North (water god). *Authors' collections.*

BOK KAI: THE WATER GOD

Bok Kai in known in Marysville as the God of the Dark North or Dark Northern Heaven. In Mandarin, he is called Bei Ti and in Cantonese and/or Taishanese, Bok Dai.

He is the water god, and his position in the Temple of Many Saints is appropriate due to the fact that the building and Bok Kai are situated facing Yuba River, which periodically brings threats of flooding during the wet seasons. It is said that some of Bok Kai's powers are to oversee irrigational waterways and rain. He also has the power to control fire, summon rain and regulate water flow. He is seen as a preventer of floods and fire.

Bok Kai was once human and was promoted to heaven because of his good deeds. One of the oldest stories places him in the Hsia Dynasty more than four thousand years ago. He was credited with controlling water and introducing flood control through the construction of drainage, ditches and levees.

He was a great warrior, and his most dramatic deed occurred near the end of Shang Dynasty and the beginning of the Chou Dynasty. It was the defeat of Wo Wang, the Demon King. Wo Wang came to earth to destroy mankind. As Wo Wang was causing destruction of mankind, the primal deity Yuan Shih T'ien ordered the Jade Emperor to appoint Bok Kai to combat Wo Wang.

Bok Kai was given a dozen heavenly armies to fight Wo Wang and his demon armies. Bok Kai entered the conflict and fought the demon armies with his hair flowing over his shoulders, wearing a black robe with a golden breastplate. He fought barefoot amid dark lowering clouds, raising a black sacred banner in the midst of the black flags of his troops in battle.

Wo Wang summoned evil spirits, a gray tortoise and a gigantic serpent, to destroy Bok Kai, but they instead were defeated by him. Bok Kai then cast all the demons into the abyss. After his victory, the gray tortoise and the gigantic serpent became Bok Kai's attendants.

Following the battle, Bok Kai returned to the calm skies and was given the title Yuan T'ien Shang Ti, or First Lord of Heaven. He is shown on the altar with his right foot on top of the gray tortoise and the left foot on top of the gigantic serpent.

QUAN YING: THE GODDESS OF MERCY

Quan Ying (Guanyin, Gone Yim or Kuan Yin) is the first deity on the left on the main altar. This goddess also goes by the names Quan Am in Vietnam, Kwan Eim in Thailand and Kwan Um in Korea.

She is the Chinese Goddess of Mercy, Compassion and Kindness. She is the most well-known goddess in China and liked by both young and old people. Her name means "One who gazes down upon the world and hears the cries of the people." She is probably the most valued and honored of all the gods among the Chinese.

Quan Ying is often the only Buddhist on a Taoist altar and is the Chinese version of the Indian Buddhist deity Avalokitesvara. She is a bodhisattva, one who has achieved enlightenment but refused to enter Nirvana (and become a true Buddha) out of compassion for the suffering beings. While no bodhisattva has gender, Chinese usually think of her as being female—especially concerned for women and children, immensely powerful, benevolent, loving and venerated by just about everyone, from Buddhists to Taoists and even agnostics. Today, a great many Westerners have also discovered this goddess and taken her to heart.

Quan Ying, the Goddess of Mercy. *Authors' collections.*

Quan Gung: The God of War and Peace

Quan Gung (Qwan Kung, Quan Yu, Guan-Yun-Chang, Guan-Gong or Chang-Sheng), second from the left on the main altar, was known as the God of War and Peace, as well as of Literature and Valor. He is depicted as a fierce-looking man with a red face and a black beard, sometimes shown holding either a book or halberd.

He was once a living person (a military hero in AD 184) and was the most popular among early immigrants to America from Guangzhou. He demonstrated not only military valor but also loyalty, high principles and justice. He was a top military advisor and warrior who exercised bravery and fair play.

He was even known to have sacrificed his personal success when it would have required him to compromise his principles. He was a mighty warrior and the destroyer of evil and is often displayed by businesses as a sign of trustworthiness and a defender of their good name.

He is highly regarded by businesspeople, police and martial arts devotees, among others. He is often associated with wealth and is the only god depicted with a red face; he is sometimes depicted with his Black Dragon Sword and is the keeper of good people and fights those who might harm them. These qualities are the reasons he was venerated after his death and became very popular among the early Cantonese who came to America.

Quan Gung, the God of War and Peace. *Authors' collections.*

YUK FUNG: THE SECRETARY OF STATE GOD

Yuk Fung (Yu-Huang, Yu-Huang-Shandi, Yu-Huang-Shang-Ti, Tian-Gong, Tien-Kung, Tai Ing, Yu Feng or Yü Ti), second from the right on the main altar, is a god that holds the position of Secretary of State for civic and military activities. He is thought to govern heaven and earth and was considered the supreme god of law, order, justice and creation. He gave the people culture, architecture, skill in battle and agriculture and was worshiped during the Shang Dynasty (1600–1046 BC).

He is also known as the Great Holy Father, the God of Justice, the Highest Emperor, Yellow Emperor or Yu Huang Shang-Ti. He is the one who is invested with the Jade symbol. As the Jade Emperor, he was considered to be the ruler of heaven and controls all gods from the other religions.

He is the highest deity in Taoism and the most revered and popular of Chinese deities. His responsibilities include keeping everything in harmony and regulating peace and war. He is the great organizer of the universe and guides human affairs by straightening out much of the confusion in heaven. In the temple, he is shown with a black face.

Yuk Fung, the Secretary of State God.
Authors' collections.

SING MOO: THE GODDESS FOR SAFE TRAVEL

Sing Moo (T'ien-Hou or Sheng-Mu), first on the right on the main altar, is a Chinese goddess who is generally worshiped by seamen or ocean travelers for a safe journey. She is also known as the Empress or Queen of Heaven and is a semi-historical figure of the tenth century who became a goddess through her virtue and her power to save sailors from storms at sea.

When seamen lose their course or are unexpectedly attacked by wind and waves and darkening clouds, they pray devoutly to Sing Moo, and she is always ready to hear their pleas. She may often be seen standing in the skies, dividing the wind with her sword. When she does this, the wind departs for the North and South, and the waves grow smooth.

She is the patron of seafarers, including fishermen and sailors; her worship spread throughout China's coastal regions and Chinese communities throughout Southeast Asia. She was thought to roam the seas, protecting her believers through miraculous interventions.

In America, she was probably the second-most popular deity among early Chinese. It is believed that her placement in the temple is in gratitude for the thousands of Chinese arriving safely to America after the long journey from China across the Pacific Ocean.

Sing Moo, the Goddess for Safe Travel. *Authors' collections.*

WA HO: THE GOD OF HEALTH OR SURGERY

Wa Ho (Hau T'o, Hau Tuo or Yuan Hua) is the God of Health or Surgery. He has his own altar to the left of the main altar. He was also considered the God of Medicine. He was a famous Chinese physician associated with healing of illness and injury during the late Eastern Han Dynasty (AD 25–220). He was so famous that his name and image adorn numerous products and a frequently used acupuncture point. He was considered the first surgeon of China and one of the last famous surgeons of ancient China.

The records of the Three Kingdoms and book of the Later Han showed that he was the first person in China to use anesthesia during surgery. His ideas of surgery, acupuncture and tai chi movements had an important influence on later Chinese medicine and led to his coming to be seen as a god within a few centuries of his death. He is sometimes shown holding a bottle or gourd containing herbal medicine.

People worship Wa Ho for the healing of illness and injury.

Wa Ho, the God of Health or Surgery. *Authors' collections.*

OTHER GODS IN THE TEMPLE

There are other gods worshiped in the Bok Kai Temple. Some of these gods are listed on the brass tablet in front of the main altar. The year 1880 is inscribed on the tablet.

Gum Far (aka Jin Hua or Gold Flower Lady) works as a midwife. Expectant mothers seek advice and comfort from her. She was a southern Chinese virgin deity who was popular among women in seventeenth-century Guangzhou (Canton). She has traditionally been sought out by women for issues related to children's health, including pregnancy, delivery and pediatric problems.

Tu Di (aka Tudigong or Tudishen) is the earth god or God of the Soil and Ground. He performs the function of protecting the community against hazards such as drought and fire; mass worship in crisis or at festivals during normal times served as rallying occasions to heighten the community consciousness of the local population. Although rarely the main deity of any Taoist temple, he is present as a statue or a name on a tablet in almost all of them. Shrines of Tu Di are everywhere—in homes, shops, temples and even cemeteries, often located directly on the ground. He is depicted as an elderly, well-dressed man with a calm smile and a peaceful pose, usually seated. In California, he seems to have had special importance among miners. This may be because, as god of all things in the ground, he controls deposits of minerals, including gold.

Ts'ai Shen (aka Choy Bok Sing Quan, Fu Ts-'ai or Cai Shen) is the God of Wealth and Luck and is often worshiped during the Chinese New Year celebrations. He was one of the most popular gods of ancient China and is widely believed to bestow on his devotees the riches carried around by him. He was not only the god of material wealth but also of a rich life, which meant a happy family and a secure, successful and respectable trade. Ts'ai Shen was very generous to his followers but was not foolish. People had to prove themselves worthy of his generosity by working hard, praying to him regularly and thanking him for his gifts. He oversees the gaining and distribution of wealth through fortune and is displayed in Chinese businesses and homes around the world.

Hoo Gee (aka How Toe or Tu Di Gong) is known as the protective God of Earth. He protects a local place (especially hills), and his statue may be found at roadside shrines. He is also the God of Wealth, by virtue of his connection with the earth and, therefore, minerals and buried treasure.

When people come to the temple to worship, they come to worship the gods and seek guidance in many different situations. There is a general awareness among the worshipers that positive direction is given to them, and they are satisfied with the results.

Chapter 5
THE MARYSVILLE DRAGONS

THE FIRST MARYSVILLE DRAGON

The first Marysville's Chinese Dragon was the best-known dragon in America from the 1880s to the early 1900s. It was called Moo Lung, which translates to Dancing Dragon. It was sometimes referred to as Gum Lung, or Golden Dragon.

In 1878, Marysville's Chinatown had a fairly large Chinese population and was able to secure the dragon crafted by artisans in China. The intricate, detailed dragon head is made up of papier-mâché, silk, hand-blown glass and kingfisher feathers. The body is made of richly colored cloth, embroidered and spangled with intricate designs.

Moo Lung was the first ceremonial dragon brought to America in 1878 and cost between $5,000 to $7,000. It was 150 feet long, and over the years, due to wear and tear, the dragon was reduced to 100 feet in length. One hundred dancers were required to carry him in the parade.

In addition, there were three or four other performers employed to prance in front of the dragon, waving in front of it on a pole an orb of a fish or pearl intended to tease him into writhing. It performed from the 1880s onward and retired in 1916. Moo Lung came out of retirement and performed in 1930 and 1931 for the Bomb Day celebrations. Universal Newsreel Company in 1931 covered the event for presentation in movie theaters throughout the United States and other countries.

The Chinese character for dragon (Lung). *Authors' collections.*

Moo Lung is being set up for the 1895 Bomb Day parade. *Courtesy Bing Ong.*

Moo Lung was loaned one more time to San Francisco in 1937 for the colorful Jade Festival to raise funds for the hospital in Chinatown. After that, only the dragon head remained and was stored and displayed in the Council Chamber at the Bok Kai Temple.

To fully understand the significance of the Marysville Dragon, one needs to understand the history of dragons. Dragons have long been a symbol in Chinese folklore and art. There are documents in China that note that the presence of dragons dates back to the fifth millennium BC during the Yangshao culture in Henan, estimated at between 5000 BC and 3000 BC. As the emblem of past emperors and the imperial command, the legend of the Chinese dragon is used as a symbol of imperial strength and power.

Over time, the dragon in Chinese culture has come to be regarded as a creature with the power to bless, influence lives and scare off evil spirits. Chinese dragons traditionally symbolize potent and auspicious powers, particularly control over water, rainfall, typhoons and floods.

The Chinese people have held a great respect for the dragon for centuries. Traditional Chinese legend has it that people are descendants of this powerful and mystical animal, and it is considered to be good luck to the Chinese people in terms of fertility, social graces and prosperity.

Unlike the negative energies associated with many Western dragons, Chinese dragons are beautiful, friendly and wise. Their benevolence signifies greatness, goodness and blessings. A dragon overcomes obstacles until success is his. He is energetic, decisive, optimistic, intelligent and ambitious. Many Chinese cities have pagodas where people used to burn incense and pray to dragons. The Chinese dragon is looked upon as the ultimate symbol of good fortune.

During festivals and celebrations, the Chinese believe that the dragon performance drives away evil spirits and ushers in good luck and blessings for the community—the longer the dragon is used in a celebration, the more luck it will bring to the community.

Before a dragon could be used for the first performance in a celebration, the dragon must go through a sighting ceremony to give it eyesight. This is necessary in order for the dragon to bring good luck to the community. This process is referred to as "receiving sight" and must take place on the same day the dragon is used for the first time. The ceremony begins with the burning of paper representing money to attract attention of the gods so they will come and bless the dragon. This gives the dragon life, good luck and fortune. It is then baptized with leaves from the Chinese grapefruit tree for good luck and longevity. Red dye is patted on the eyes and places on the head, blinding the dragon to all but good luck. Afterward, blossoms and streamers are placed on the head.

For any Chinese community to have a dragon participate in its celebrations would be the ultimate honor, but the cost to purchase one was usually prohibitive. The Chinese communities from the gold rush period to the first part of the 1900s were closely connected together, which indicates the existence of a network and a degree of cooperation between them. The Marysville Dragon, Moo Lung, was well known to all Chinese communities across America, and they were able to borrow Moo Lung for their celebrations.

Among some of the Chinese communities that borrowed Moo Lung were San Francisco (1885 and 1937), Oakland (1907), Chicago (1893), Los Angeles (1896 and 1902), Red Bluff (1908), Santa Rosa (1909), Seattle (1909) and New York (1911 and 2014). The Chinese community of Cleveland requested to borrow the dragon for its 1910 Fourth of July celebration, but due to scheduling conflict, the Marysville Chinese community was unable to fulfill that request.

CHINESE DRAGON IS IN GREAT DEMAND

Ah Fee, the Chinese merchant who is custodian of the "dragon," which belongs to the local Celestial colony, says that a countryman of his, a leading spirit in the Chinatown of Cleveland, Ohio, is here. The object of his visit is to get the dragon for the Fourth of July in the Ohio city on Lake Erie. Ah Fee notified him that the dragon had been secured for the anniversary celebration in Marysville.

It is the only one in the United States and cost a small fortune. It has been loaned at different times to Sacramento, Los Angeles, San Francisco and other California cities on different fete days and was one of the principal features in the opening parade of the Alaskan-Yukon exposition at Seattle.

Ah Fee is wedded to his adopted city of Marysville and the offer of money failed to shake his loyalty to the county seat of Yuba. By the way the Chinese division in the Fourth of July parade will be one of the features of the day. Their different societies, and they have lots of them, will be in life and when it comes to uniforms they are resplendent with all the colors of the rainbow, and their antequated swords, guns and battleaxes look as though they dated back to about the time old Noah was monarch of all he surveyed.

Article in the *Marysville Daily Appeal*, July 6, 1910. *Courtesy California State Library.*

Moo Lung is shown here in San Francisco's Chinatown parading on Washington Street. The Marysville Dragon in San Francisco was referred to as Gum Lung. *Courtesy University of California–Berkeley, Bancroft Library.*

Poster advertising the 1893 Columbian Exposition in Chicago, also known as the Chicago World's Fair. *Authors' collections.*

Moo Lung in San Francisco Parades

Moo Lung was loaned to San Francisco's Chinese community for its parade in 1885. In 1937, Moo Lung was brought out of retirement and loaned once again to San Francisco and used in the Jade Festival to raise funds for a Chinese hospital. For this event, due to wear and tear, it was only one hundred feet in length. The parade was a huge success, with people lined up throughout Chinatown on the parade route.

Moo Lung in the Chicago World Fair

When Moo Lung was loaned to the Chicago Chinese community to perform at the 1893 Columbian Exposition in Chicago (the World's Fair), there were objections from the white community over the use of the dragon. However, surprisingly, in spite of those objections, Moo Lung turned out to be a popular attraction with most whites. The dragon performance at the fair may have been the first to be aimed mainly at a non-Chinese audience.

Moo Lung in Los Angeles

The Chinese community in Los Angeles borrowed Moo Lung twice, for the La Fiesta de Los Angeles parades in 1896 and again in 1902.

Moo Lung to Red Bluff

The June 24, 1908 *Red Bluff Daily News* reported the borrowing of the Marysville Dragon:

> *There was rejoicing yesterday amongst the Chinese residents of Red Bluff. Good tidings had come from the south, and it spelled the success of the Chinese representation for the big Fourth of July parade. The great Chinese dragon will be in the parade. This dragon, which will require some seventy carriers, belongs to Marysville, and there is only one dragon in California as large. The latter is in San Francisco, which city it never leaves. The Chinese of Marysville are more liberal with their monster, and upon sundry other occasions it has been loaned to cities of Central California. But it has*

Moo Lung in Los Angeles in the La Fiesta Parade in 1902. *Courtesy California Historical Society Collection, University of Southern California Digital Library.*

never been as far north as Red Bluff before. The local Chinese colony are pleased with the idea of joining in the Fourth of July celebration, and they appreciate the committee's Invitation.

MOO LUNG IN SEATTLE

Moo Lung was loaned to Seattle for its Alaska Yukon Pacific Exposition in 1909. As noted in the *Seattle Post-Intelligencer*, the local newspaper, the great parade dragon that formed the center of attention on China Day was borrowed, not locally owned. Chinese communities in America were closely connected and could usually be counted on to help other communities. In the case of the dragon, it was the rich gold rush town of Marysville, California, that agreed to lend Seattle one of the largest and finest dragons in America, 150 feet in length and needing sixty strong men to carry it.

Accordingly, it was brought from Marysville in sections "at great expense," as reported in the newspaper, and assembled in the afternoon before the China Day parades. The Marysville Dragon was a smashing success.

Moo Lung parading down Fifth Avenue in downtown Seattle. *Courtesy University of Washington Libraries Digital Collections.*

Non-Chinese children squealed and clapped their hands. White onlookers cheered. Moo Lung handlers, praised for their enthusiasm and endurance, sweated inside.

The *Seattle Times* newspaper reported on the dragon and parades extensively, for once without a trace of prejudice or patronizing attitudes. No one threw stones or, as far as is known, shouted racial epithets. White and Chinese leaders mingled as apparent equals. And everyone, Chinese, whites and other Seattle ethnicities, were said to have enjoyed themselves.

MOO LUNG IN NEW YORK

For the Fourth of July Parade of Nations in 1911 in New York, the *New York Times* wrote the following on the Marysville's Chinese dragon:

> *The large and prosperous community of Chinese residents in Marysville, California acquired this ceremonial dragon from China in the 1878. The majestic "Moo Lung" appeared in parades and celebrations nationwide, including the July 4th, 1911 "Parade of Nations" in New York City.*

Moo Lung was loaned to New York Chinese community for their Fourth of July Parade of Nations in 1911. *Courtesy Library of Congress.*

MOO LUNG RETURNS TO NEW YORK

In March 2014, the New-York Historical Society Museum and Library requested to borrow Moo Lung for display in the Historical Society's Chinese American: Exclusion/Inclusion Exhibit. The exhibit focused on the experiences of Chinese in America and integrated this history into a broader history of the United States.

In exchange, the New York Historical Society Museum and Library agreed to pay for the professional restoration and conservation of the dragon head. Since Moo Lung has been idle and in storage since 1937, extensive restoration of Moo Lung was required before it could be displayed.

Moo Lung's body is long gone, and now only the head remains. The internal framework structure looked like spaghetti, as it seems like the people who previously repaired it may not have had the time or patience. Much of the work was cleaning and repairing the structure. Most of the bamboo framework, fastened with twisted paper ties and wire, was preserved, Moo Lung's entire head was very dirty and needed to be redone. There were more than a dozen bells tied under Moo Lung's head that required work. These made noise as the

Moo Lung on display at the Bok Kai Temple after being returned in 2015 from the New-York Historical Society Museum and Library. *Authors' collections.*

dragon was maneuvered down the street. The tongue and jaw had completely detached from the head.

Hundreds of tiny mirrors and accompanying brass frames needed cleaning to have them more easily visible. Fully restored, the predominantly green dragon head stood at least six feet tall.

After the restoration effort, Moo Lung was displayed at the New York Historical Society Museum and Library from September 2014 to May 2015. It was a highlight of the exhibit, conveying the history of the Bok Kai Temple and the Marysville Chinese community, the rich cultural life that Chinese Americans maintained from the early years and the participation of Chinese Americans in community and civic events throughout the country.

DRAGONS AFTER MOO LUNG

There have been four dragons since the first dragon, Moo Lung (1878–1916). All the subsequent dragons were similar to Moo Lung, made of richly colored material, embroidered and spangled with intricate designs. The heads of the dragons were constructed from a wood frame with papier-mâché, silk and other material. Two horns embellish the heads, with mirrors and bells on their foreheads to scare away evil spirits. A head can weigh up to one hundred pounds. The body of the dragon consists of the skin or covering over the bones or frame. The skin is made from silk or cloth material and covered with scales. Traditionally, the structure is made of bamboo supported by wooden poles. Later, some dragon structures were made of aluminum to reduce the weight.

SECOND DRAGON
Kim Lung (Golden Dragon)
Parade from 1969 until 1984
120 feet long
Cost $1,500 in 1969
A surplus dragon purchased from San Francisco Chinese Chamber of Commerce

THIRD DRAGON
Kim Lung II (Golden Dragon II)
Parade from 1985 until 1991
150 feet long
Cost $5,000 in 1985
Dragon made in Kowloon, China

FOURTH DRAGON
Lung Huang (Dragon King)
Parade from 1991 to 2009
152 feet long
Cost $10,000 in 1991
Dragon made in Hong Kong

FIFTH DRAGON
Hong Wan Lung or Fook Lung (Luck Dragon)
Parade from 2009 to the present

Hong Wan Lung, the present dragon, debuted in 2009, replacing Lung Huang in the Bomb Day celebration in 2009. *Authors' collections.*

Lung Huang (fourth dragon) is encircled by Hong Wan Lung (fifth dragon) at the bottom of the picture, with its tail in the upper right of the picture. *Authors' collections.*

175 feet long
Cost $15,000 in 2009
Dragon made in Hong Kong

At the Bok Kai Festival celebration in 2009, Hong Wan Lung was brought to life and made its debut, performing together with Lung Huang during the parade celebration before the latter was retired. This is the only time in history of the Bok Kai Festival that two dragons performed together in the parade.

A Marysville Dragon had been parading in Marysville during the Bok Kai Festival since the acquisition of Moo Lung in 1878 until retiring; the subsequent dragons were used from 1969 to the present day. In the early years, with a large Chinese population in Marysville and the surrounding communties of several thousand Chinese, performers for the dragon were all Chinese. However, over the years, the Chinese population started declining, and by 1960, there were fewer than four hundred Chinese in Marysville and the surrounding area. The Chinese in Marysville were no longer able to continue parading the dragon without help from outside the Chinese community.

Since the current dragon requires sixty or more people to carry it, the airmen at the Beale Air Force Base (formerly known as Camp Beale) volunteered to perform that function, bringing the dragon to life and marching in the Bok Kai Parade from 1969 to present.

Beale Air Force Base is located eight miles southeast of Marysville and was established in October 1942 as a training site for the Thirteenth Armored and the Eighty-First and Ninety-Sixth Infantry Divisions. During World War II, the military base's eighty-six thousand acres were home to more than sixty thousand soldiers, a prisoner of war encampment and a one-thousand-bed hospital. The relationship between the Beale Air Force Base and the Bok Kai Parade goes back to the 1960s.

During the Bok Kai Parades, people would line the parade route, awaiting the arrival of the dragon. As the dragon began its journey on the parade route, there would be performers who would light firecrackers ahead of the dragon to ward off any evil spirits and to announce the approach. This would generate a sense of excitement, and children's faces would light up at the first sign of the dragon. It was quite a sight to behold as the dragon pranced in a serpentine path along the street, being teased by several performers in front and the children screaming (from excitement rather than fear). Although the dragon's appearance is both frightening and bold, there is a benevolent feeling that is projected from the dragon and felt by the spectators. As in all the Bok Kai celebrations, the performance of the dragon is the highlight of the parade.

Chapter 6

THE BOK KAI FESTIVAL (BOMB DAY)

The Bok Kai Festival is celebrated to honor Bok Kai, the water god. One version of the origin of the festival has Wo Wang, the Demon King, out to destroy mankind; Bok Kai was summoned by the Jade Emperor to oppose Wo Wang. Bok Kai defeated the Demon King even after he summoned a gray tortoise and a gigantic serpent to fight for him. After Bok Kai's victory, the gray tortoise and the gigantic serpent became his attendants; Bok Kai is shown in the temple with his right foot on top of the gray tortoise and the left foot on top of the gigantic serpent.

The Bok Kai Festival is the celebration of Bok Kai's victory. The early Bok Kai Festival drew the Chinese from the gold mines of the Sierra Nevada and the cities of Sacramento, San Francisco and other nearby Chinese communities to celebrate and worship at the Bok Kai Temple.

According to Daniel Kim, a native of Marysville and nephew of Joe Lung Kim, a prior caretaker of the Bok Kai Temple, "Thousands of people have come through here during the festival. We have had people from Seattle, Portland, Denver, Hawaii and even Hong Kong. And they're very serious about it. They come to pray and to give an offering. There's no other place in the world that has this type of celebration."

The name Bomb Day derives from the firing of bombs on Sunday at 4:00 p.m. that contain "good fortune" rings. The Chinese called the firing of the bombs "Sell Pow." In the past, the firing of bombs for Chinese celebrations was very common in China. This practice was brought over from China and was performed in many gold rush Chinatowns in Northern California such as

The Bok Kai Festival poster for 1985, the year of the Ox. It is the year 4683 on the Chinese lunar calendar. *Authors' collections.*

Watsonville, Oroville, Yreka and Grass Valley. Grass Valley ended the firing of bombs in 1919, and Watsonville ended the firing of bombs by 1925. After 1925, only Marysville and Oroville continued, and Oroville stopped shortly afterward. Marysville is the only place in the United States where the firing of bombs for celebrations is now performed.

There is no official date for when the celebration began. Some scholars noted that it could be as early as 1869. The *Marysville Daily Appeal* newspaper of February 29, 1869, mentioned a bomb festival but did not provide any details. The March 14, 1873 edition of the *Marysville Weekly Appeal* had the best description of the firing of the bomb:

ARYSVILLE, CALIFORNIA

ANOTHER HOLIDAY

The Chinese residents of the city belonging to the See Up Company, participated yesterday afternoon in another religious holiday. The religious ceremonies took place at the Josh Temple....The religions services terminated in the Temple at half-past 2 o'clock, when a procession was formed on the street, headed by music and banners and led by the priest up First Street to the foot of Virgin Alley, the place selected for the discharge of sixteen bombs, each containing a trophy entitling the catcher, as it descended, to certain privileges during the next six months. The priest with drawn sword, blessed the grounds where the contest was to take place and about seventy-five stout and young Chinamen stripped for the tussle. The sixteen bombs were discharged at intervals of a few minutes and a vigorous contest following for the trophy as it descended. It was rough and tumble work. They fought for it as if their lives depended on the result. This was witnessed by at least a thousand Chinamen and about one hundred Melican men.

Some of the earlier festivals involved an extensive parade with many floats followed by Moo Lung, the famous Marysville Dragon. This is considered the oldest continuous parade in California. The Bok Kai Festival is the largest event in Marysville.

In the earlier celebrations, the participants were all Chinese. In 1930, the Chinese observed Bomb Day jointly with the City of Marysville for the first time. But with a declining Chinese population in Marysville, the involvement of the whole community increased, and the name was changed to the Bok Kai Festival in the mid-1950s.

As the Chinese population started declining, fewer and fewer Chinese-related activities were taking place, and more community-wide activities were replacing them, such as a vendors' fair, a 5K run, an art show, a fashion show, piano concerts and a children's activity area.

Although the elder Chinese still consider it a religious event with significant spiritual importance, the wider community considers it more of a historical and cultural event to honor the Chinese in the Marysville area.

During the celebration from the late 1800s to the mid-1900s, an open house would prevail at the Suey Sing Tong Association and Hop Sing Tong Association, and the public was invited to lunch and dinner, which went on all day long and into the evening. Food was plentiful and cheap in those days, and the revenue derived from the gambling table at the tong associations paid for everything.

The gambling game played was an ancient Chinese game with a set of thirty-two Chinese dominoes. It was a fast-moving game that the Chinese call it Pai Gow. Pai Gow played during the festival had no one set banker. It was conducted in rotation, with each player receiving a chance to be the boss of a hand, provided he had enough capital to cover all bets. Each winner of each hand was taxed 5 percent of his winnings, which went to the tong association. From the 1920s to the 1940s, it was not uncommon to see $100 bills on the table on each deal. During the festival, a tong association could pick up $40,000 to $50,000. This would pay for all expenses for the tongs for a whole year and still provide free food for the public.

The present format of the festival is a two-day event on the weekend, following the second day of the second month on the lunar calendar. The parade and most festival activities are on the first day. The main event for the second day was the firing of the bombs at 4:00 p.m. at First and C Streets, the center of Chinatown.

Before the festival, Chinatown is dressed up for the celebration. Bright-colored ribbons, flags and banners with Chinese characters denoting well wishes and good luck are hung from the balconies of buildings, on poles and at the temple, creating a very festive atmosphere in Chinatown.

Parade banners are set out at front of the Bok Kai Temple for the festival in the late 1890s. *Courtesy Gordon Tom.*

Suey Sing Tong Association Building at First and C Streets is decorated for the Bok Kai Festival in the 1920s. *Courtesy Gordon Tom.*

Pearl Lim, Bertha Waugh, Helen Jang and Helen Yee dressed up in traditional Chinese dresses (*cheongsam* in Chinese) for the 1938 Bok Kai Festival. *Courtesy Brenda Lee Wong.*

Above: Firecrackers are unpacked to be set up for firing. *Courtesy Bing Ong.*

Right: Firecrackers are hung from the balcony of the Suey Sing Tong Building to be lit during the celebration. *Courtesy Bing Ong.*

In addition, many of the young girls in Chinatown are dressed up in traditional Chinese dresses.

During the celebration, massive numbers of firecrackers are exploded around Chinatown, and before long, the residue will have turned the streets in Chinatown magenta.

The 1930, the Bok Kai Festival was a well-publicized event. A series of stories regarding the festival in the *Sutter Independent* newspaper began several days in advance to promote and attract people into Marysville. The *Appeal Democrat* provided front-page coverage of the festival on March 1, 1930. In the following issue on March 3, the newspaper reported that six motion picture newsreel companies were represented in Marysville on Saturday and Sunday, making sound and silent pictures of the Chinese celebration. It also reported that Paramount Studios had its elaborately equipped car here and took 850 feet of film of the parade and 350 feet of the bomb firing. The newspaper felt that through the newsreel services, the newspapers and the amateur photographers, the community would get an immense amount of publicity all over the world. The famous dragon Moo Lung that had been retired in 1916 was brought out to perform in the parade.

In 1931, the Universal Newsreel Company covered the event and released one-minute film clips to show in movie theaters across the country and several

1931 Bok Kai Parade on First Street being filmed by Universal Newsreel Company. *Courtesy Brenda Lee Wong.*

Chinese opera performers in the Suey Sing Tong Association Building in 1947 during the Bok Kai Festival. The musicians are to the right. *Courtesy Gordon Tom.*

foreign countries. Moo Lung was again brought out at this celebration to perform in the parade.

As part of the Bomb Day celebration in 1931, the famous Chinese opera star sisters Misses Hom York Lum and Hom Suey Fong, as well as other noted Chinese opera singers and actresses, were hired to perform at the event. They were brought in from San Francisco with a $30,000 bond and an assurance for their "safe return." It was noted in the local newspaper that they were "being brought to Marysville through arrangements with the Mandarin Theater in San Francisco at considerable cost to the local Chinese."

The lion dance is a very important part of any Chinese celebration and has been part of the Chinese culture for thousands of years. The lion dance originated during the Tang Dynasty (AD 618–906). It represents power, wisdom and good fortune and brings longevity and good luck.

The lion dance is done along with the lighting of firecrackers, the clashing of cymbals and the playing of drums. The noise was believed to scare negative and evil spirits away. In addition to performing in the parade, the lion dance performers would visit the shops in the community to perform the traditional custom of "Cai Qing," meaning "plucking the greens." Strings of green lettuce with money in red envelopes are tied together and hung

Lily Dong is next to the lion in front of the Suey Sing Tong building at the Bok Kai celebration, circa the 1920s. *Courtesy Brenda Lee Wong.*

Above: The lion dance in front of Suey Sing Tong Association, circa the 1940s. *Courtesy Gene Sing Lim.*

Right: The festival lion is dancing in front of the Suey Sing Tong Building, ready for "Cai Qing," circa the 1940s. *Courtesy Gene Sing Lim.*

Ella Kim being crowned as the Queen of Bomb Day in 1947. *Courtesy Virginia Ong.*

Four of the eight contestants for the Queen at the 1947 Bomb Day Dance in traditional Chinese dresses: Clare Waugh, Virginia Ong, Ella Kim and Mary Ong. *Courtesy Virginia Ong.*

from the doorway or balcony of an establishment. The lion while dancing would seize the lettuce and the red envelope with the money with its mouth and "spit" out the torn-up leaves to signify the distribution of wealth and prosperity. The money is the reward for bringing good luck and fortune to the establishment.

In addition to the lion dance, the performers would also do martial arts demonstrations since the lion dance is based on traditional kung fu footwork, kicks and stances and the performers are trained to do both.

In 1947, the Marysville Tsing Hua Club, sponsor of the Chinese Bomb day dance, initiated the first queen of Bomb Day contest. There were eight local contestants. The first Bomb Day Queen selected was Ella Kim, an eighteen-year-old Marysville High School student. She was crowned queen of Bomb Day by Harold Sperbeck, the Marysville mayor and city councilman at the Bomb Day Dance.

The parade is the highlight for Saturday's Bok Kai celebration. Each parade has a gong master who signals the start of the parade by banging a ceremonial gong along the parade route; this also wakes up the gods for the celebration. Bing Ong, a community leader in Marysville's Chinatown, was the gong master for ten years from 1990 to 2000. He was the owner of the famous Chinese restaurant Lotus Inn, located at Oak and Second Streets in Maysville.

Bing Ong as the gong master, leading off the Bok Kai Parade in 1995. *Courtesy Bing Ong.*

In the earlier parades, only the Chinese participated. The parades included Chinese dressed in traditional Chinese clothing and carrying banners, floats with Chinese displays and Moo Lung. Blessings are given by the dragon to the establishments along the way. The parade starts in Chinatown and runs up through D Street, the main commercial district in Marysville, before returning to Chinatown.

In later years, when the whole Marysville community was involved, the parade expanded to include many non-Chinese entries. There were many floats, community dignitaries, elected officials, high school marching bands, drill teams, military units, boys' and girls' Scout clubs and more.

The main event of the Bok Kai Festival on Sunday is the firing of bombs at 4:00 p.m. in the center of Chinatown at First and C Streets. The intersection is roped off by the Marysville Police Department. The firing of the bombs is the last event during the festival.

The firing of bombs in the past was very common in Chinese celebrations. Due to current regulations and safety, Marysville is one of the only places (if not the only place) in California that has permission from the California State Fire Marshal Office to manufacture and fire the bombs for the celebration. The bombs resemble giant firecrackers. Prior to 1949, all the bombs were imported from China. After the Communists took over China, the importing of the bombs ceased.

The parade float is on First Street just past C Street in 1895. *Courtesy Gordon Tom.*

Moo Lung parading on First Street in 1895. *Courtesy Bing Ong.*

Moo Lung came out of retirement for the 1930 and 1931 celebrations. Here Moo Lung is on D Street between Third and Fourth Streets. *Courtesy Bing Ong.*

The bombs are made from discarded magazines, rolled tightly around a stalk of bamboo. The rest of the process requires melted resin, dirt, gunpowder, twine and gold leaf paper. A "good luck" ring is made from fine wire. The bombs are wrapped with color paper like an oversized firecracker and packed with just the right amount of gunpowder. Each one is two inches by five inches in size. A ring is made from rope to form a circle and wrapped with a red ribbon. Each ribbon has a number, and each number corresponds to a fortune in old Chinese custom.

Jimmy Pon, the third bomb maker, holding a finished bomb. *Authors' collections.*

The first bomb maker was Tim Lim, who learned the tedious and ancient craft in his native China. John Young was the second bomb maker, from 1974 to 1981, and Jimmy Pon was the third bomb maker, from 1981 to 1993. Al Wong Jr. assumed the responsibility of making the bombs in 1993.

A special permit and license are issued each year to the Marysville Chinese community for the production of one hundred bombs. However, only ten to fifteen are now fired by the Chinese community. The rest are sold to individuals and fired during the Bok Kai Festival in Chinatown for their own pleasure.

The firing of bombs starts with a procession of Chinese elders carrying the sacred jade tablet with the names of deities from the Bok Kai Temple. They are led by a clanging gong and hundreds of exploding firecrackers, which paves the way east from the temple at First and D Streets to a roped-off intersection of First and C Streets, where several hundreds of spectators are gathered.

The elders set the sacred jade tablet on a table facing north at the intersection and, standing in front of the table, respectfully bow three times.

With arms extended, participants scramble for the good luck ring in 1947. *Courtesy Virginia Ong*

In the meantime, all the younger men (the tallest, strongest and toughest) would gather in the roped-off area. It was like rugby football!

A hollowed-out stump is moved to the center of the intersection of First and C Streets, where a bomb is inserted and lit to the constant sounding of the gong. As the bomb explodes, it sends a ring fifty to seventy-five feet into the air. Firecrackers are lit and thrown on the ground all around the young men as they rush as one mass of humanity to the center of where they figure the ring would land, all with upraised hands, hoping that the ring would fall into their hands. This can get very aggressive and violent as the participants struggle for the ring. The Marysville police are on hand to watch that the event doesn't get out of control.

The rings are generally sold to elders to return to the temple and have them blessed. This would bring good luck to the holder for the year. Each ring is numbered, and the no. 4 ring was considered the best and most sought-after ring. It was said that the person who had the no. 4 ring many years ago had his fortune increased many times, and the story remains to this day. After the firing of the bombs, the sacred jade tablet is returned to the temple, and this concludes the ceremony for the year.

The firing of bombs has been done in Marysville for more than 150 years, and many of the present-day elders still remember when their parents or grandparents brought them to Marysville to worship at the temple and watch the firing of the bombs.

Although the Bok Kai Festival is a community celebration, the Bok Kai Temple and the firing of the bombs have a spiritual meaning to the Chinese—they form the glue that keeps Marysville's Chinatown alive.

Chapter 7

CHINATOWN'S FIRST GENERATION

The first generation of Chinese pioneers who settled in Marysville were mainly from the Sze Yup counties in Guangdong Province in southern China. The people from this area are well known for being confident and adventurous. Their stubbornness is legendary. They refused to give up even when a situation appeared hopeless. These were three of the first-generation families who never gave up and settled in Marysville in the late 1800s.

JOE BONG AND LEW YUET WOON

Joe Bong and Lew Yuet Woon are the patriarch and matriarch of a remarkable Chinese American family. Their descendants include Alice Fong Yu, the first Chinese American teacher in the San Francisco School District; the Honorable Samuel Yee, one of the first Chinese American judges in California; Emma Dong, MD, the first woman to be accepted into the University of California, San Francisco Ophthalmology Department; and Collin Dong, MD, one of the first Chinese American graduates from the Stanford Medical School, a well-known doctor and author in the San Francisco Chinatown.

Joe Bong came to America in 1867 with the help of the Chinese Six Companies in San Francisco. This organization was a major force in helping the Chinese to immigrate and get established in this country. Through the financial and legal help of the Chinese Six Companies, Joe Bong obtained a land lease in Tehama County, where he started farming and was successful in growing peanuts.

In the late 1870s, Joe Bong married Lew Yuet Woon through an arranged marriage. Lew Yuet Woon came to the America in 1870

Joe Bong, 1890. *Courtesy Brenda Lee Wong.*

Lew Yuet Woon, 1890. *Courtesy Brenda Lee Wong.*

when she was only twelve years old. The couple who brought her to the America were not her parents. In China, she refused to have her feet bound, and thus she would not have been considered a respectable match for marriage in China. Her parents hoped that sending her to America would give her the opportunity to marry well, since they felt she had little chance in China. Foot binding was the custom of applying tight binding to the feet of young girls to modify the shape and size of their feet. It was practiced in China from the Tang Dynasty until the early twentieth century, and bound feet were considered a status symbol as well as a mark of beauty.

Even at an early age, she was strongwilled. She had high standards of how children should behave (according to Chinese values), and she was a strict disciplinarian. She had a temper and would use a bamboo stick to whack those who dared to disobey her.

When Lew Yuet Woon was on the peanut farm and Jennie, her daughter, was having a child and stayed in the hospital for two weeks, Lew Yuet Woon told her daughter, "I don't know why it takes so long for you to have a baby. When I had you, I just squat and had you. Your father [Joe Bong] was in the next room [and] didn't even know I had you until he heard you crying." She then said, "I just get back up and begin to cook for the farm hands."

After the peanut farm, Joe Bong and Lew Yuet Woon moved to College City in Colusa County, where he operated a laundry. After a few years, using the money he made from the laundry business, Joe Bong decided to try farming again. He moved in 1890 to Yuba City and leased a sixty-acre cherry orchard. Unfortunately, his crop was destroyed by bad weather, so he lost his entire investment.

He moved to Marysville in the 1890s and started another laundry business, and for more than fifteen years, the limited income from the laundry supported his growing family. This type of business required twelve to eighteen hours of hard labor, washing by hand and drying and ironing bundles of clothing and bedding seven days a week. As his children grew older, all were required to work in the laundry operations. Although the boys attended public school, the requirement to work in the laundry was more critical for the business to survive, so attendance in school was often cut short.

Joe Bong's life was one of hardship, as it was for many of the first-generation Chinese to America. He had the courage and strength required to survive and raise a family in America. Joe Bong and Lew Yuet Woon had three boys and three girls. Among his children's families are six physicians, a dentist and a judge. This family had truly achieved the American Dream.

HOM KUN FOO AND LEE SHEE

Hom Kun Foo and Lee Shee formed another first-generation family in Marysville. Hom Kun Foo was born in 1838 in the village of White Water (Bak Sui in Chinese) in Toishan County. The sub-village or district was known as Squid or You Yeu. He was the sixth and youngest son of Hom Tou Son and Jyu Shee. He is the twenty-eighth generation on a family tree that dates from AD 900, the Tang Dynasty.

Kun Foo was only thirteen when he left China in 1851 with an elder brother. After arriving in San Francisco, he journeyed with his brother on a riverboat to Marysville since it was the gateway to the northern mines. Here, Kun Foo found his district association and met many of his compatriots from his home county. He was able to get the latest news on the most promising mining areas. He joined a partnership that was being newly formed.

One of the advantages the Chinese had over western miners was the ability to form partnerships quickly, especially when they came from the same districts in China. In addition, Western culture is based on the individual, whereas Eastern culture is based on the group. Thus, most of the Western miners in the gold rush mined as individuals or in small partnerships. Chinese miners, on the other hand, mined in large partnerships with up to one hundred members.

They were mostly farmers from the countryside, whereas many of the Western miners were from cities. The Chinese knew how to work the soil, move water and work in the hot sun. They also had a superior diet. By drinking tea made from boiled water, they did not get sick as often as miners who drank water directly from streams and creeks. Because they knew that food was intimately connected to health, they brought much of their own food, the only immigrant group to do so.

The mining years were hard work for Kun Foo, but he persevered. After the gold ran out, he returned to Marysville in the period between the 1850s and the 1860s; he rented and later purchased the building at 310 First Street, which was his store and the home for his family for more than one hundred years. He became a major merchant in Chinatown. The store sold goods imported from China and products from local wholesalers, rice from A.F. Harris Company and general groceries from Garrett Grocery Company in Marysville.

In 1885, Kun Foo married Lee Shee from Fresno. She was from a well-to-do family. Their first son, Hom Suey Lin, was born in 1887, and over

Lee Shee and Hom
Kun Foo, 1910. *Courtesy
Gordon Tom.*

the next twenty years, they had eight more children—a total of five sons
and four daughters—all born at 310 First Street. Kun Foo had the largest
Chinese family in Marysville in 1908.

The family was growing up at a time after the passage of the Chinese
Exclusion Act, and the anti-Chinese movement was very active. The
Chinese Exclusion Act of 1882 provided that Chinese laborers, skilled and
unskilled, were absolutely excluded from immigration to American. The
act was the first law implemented to prevent all members of a specific
ethnic or national group from immigrating. This was coupled with the
growing anti-Chinese movement, led by Denis Kearney, calling for the
expulsion of all Chinese immigrants from America. "The Chinese Must
Go" was Kearney's slogan.

With these conditions, the family had to learn how to survive in an environment that was often not friendly. They understood the handicap they were under, but the Chinese are a very practical people and they learned how to adjust to the issues they encountered.

One of Kun Foo's beliefs was education for his sons. Many of them attended Chinese school, Chinese mission school and/or the Marysville public school. The public school was the most difficult because of the high level of discrimination, and the school officials discouraged or even at times prevented the Chinese from attending. In addition, other students constantly harassed them. Because of this, only one of the sons, Hom Hing (later known as Arthur Tom), the fifth son, attended the Marysville public school. The others stayed within the schools in Chinatown.

An important aspect of Kun Foo's life was his relationship with the white community. Kun Foo was very astute in his business and employed the services of an attorney, Waldo Johnson, from the white community for legal advice and to represent him when necessary. This proved invaluable over the years. He also used people in the community to verify or testify for him when necessary to prove his residency in Marysville. One of those people was the sheriff of Yuba County, Charles McCoy. Another was the U.S. mailman.

In 1910, Kun Foo started to plan a return trip to China after a fortune teller told him that he would die soon. After arriving back to his home village, he was greeted with high respect because he was the only one from that area who went to America and was not only successful but also had sons and daughters born there. He passed away in China in 1924 at the age of eighty-five.

Among his children's families, most of them completed a college education. The families include medical doctors, dentists, professors, teachers, engineers, attorneys, an elected official, pharmacists and more.

Although there were difficulties at times caused by discrimination, the third and subsequent generations were pioneers in breaking the barriers in higher education, employment and politics. Kun Foo and Lee Shee's families fully assimilated into American life and achieved the American Dream.

In 2005, the descendants of Hom Kun Foo and Lee Shee had a family reunion in Marysville. The planning started in 2004 with representatives from the eight branches of the family. All of the second generation had passed on, and the third generation was getting older. The group felt that a reunion would give the younger generations the history of the family life from the 1920s to the 1950s.

Hom Kun Foo and Lee Shee family in 1905, with a baby born in 1908 added to the photograph in 1909. *Authors' collections.*

Hom Kun Foo and Lee Shee family reunion in 2005 in Marysville—163 of the 250 family members attended. *Authors' collections.*

Even though only one member of the Hom Kun Foo and Lee Shee family is living in Marysville, the committee felt that it would still be appropriate to have the reunion there, as it was the place where Hom Kun Foo and Lee Shee first settled and started a family. In attendance were 163 members of the family, and the oldest was Herbert Gee, great-grandson of Hom Kun Foo and Lee Shee. He was ninety-three. The reunion made the front page of the local newspaper, the *Appeal Democrat*, on May 14, 2005.

ONG TALL AND LEE TOY YOKE

Ong Tall and Lee Toy Yoke settled in Marysville and opened the Kings Inn Restaurant in the center of Chinatown at First and C Streets in Marysville in the 1920s.

Ong Tall was well known in China and in America when he settled in Marysville. When General Tsai Ting Kai was visiting America in 1934 on a goodwill tour to raise funds for the war against Japan, the general and his wife were the guests of Ong Tall in Marysville. General Kai was the commander in charge of the Nineteenth Route Army, which fought against the Japanese invaders of China in the Shanghai War of 1932.

In 1939, the Chinese in America had an opportunity to change their negative image created by biased newspaper reporting. The Golden Gate International Exposition was being planned for 1939, to be held at San Francisco's Treasure Island. It would be a world's fair celebrating, among other things, the city's two newly built bridges, the Golden Gate Bridge and the San Francisco–Oakland Bay Bridge.

A Chinese village of one city block was planned where Chinese Americans could present their vision of an idealized Chinese world. The Chinese in Marysville responded. Ong Tall was commissioned to design and construct the Chinese Temple of Heaven building on Treasure Island. He received many accolades for his design.

The Chinese village was a great success, as it presented a new vision of the Chinese to visitors who had been deceived by the stereotypes of the San Francisco Chinatown as a ghetto of gambling halls, opium dens and brothels.

From the 1930s to the 1950s, Ong Tall owned several gambling halls. The gambling halls were behind legitimate operations of an antique store,

Ong Tall (*left*) with General Tsai Ting Kai and his wife, 1934. *Courtesy Virginia Ong.*

a soda fountain, a cigar store and a restaurant. These included New Paris (Mee Wah) Soda Fountain, Nanking Antique Company and the New China Club. He was very successful in his operations and purchased the former building of the local newspaper, the *Appeal Democrat*, at Second and Oak Streets. The *Appeal Democrat* was formed from the 1926 merger of two earlier newspapers, the *Marysville Appeal* (founded in 1860) and the *Marysville Evening Democrat* (founded in 1884).

Ong Tall opened the Lotus Inn in 1947 at that location. Although the upscale restaurant operations just broke even, the bar did quite well and received an award in December 1966 from Seagram's for selling 2,500 cases of its Seagram's 7 Crown liquor. The bar became a local gathering place for local politicians to socialize after their formal meetings.

Since the surrounding farmland in Marysville was a hunting ground for ducks and pheasants, many celebrities such as Bing Crosby, Roy Rogers, Richard Boone, Robert Stack, "Shakey" Johnson (of Shakey's Pizza) and others would venture into Marysville during hunting season and frequent the Lotus Inn. Among Ong Tall's collection of celebrity photographs is Roy Rogers playing the piano at the restaurant.

After Ong Tall retired, his son, Bing, continued the success of the Lotus Inn until the restaurant was purchased by the City of Marysville in 1976 for the construction of a new library parking lot. The restaurant was a member of World-Famous Restaurant International, the highest honor a restaurant can receive.

Ong Tall was one of the four major contributors to the Chinese school located at 226 First Street in 1945. He had two daughters and one son.

These were three of the first generations in Marysville that established the foundation for the future generations to succeed.

Chapter 8

CHINATOWN'S NEXT GENERATIONS

ACHIEVING THE AMERICAN DREAM

In 1870, the total population of Marysville was 4,738. The population of the Chinese in Marysville reached a peak of 1,417, about 30 percent of the total population. These were almost all male immigrants. Due to very few Chinese women in Marysville during the period from 1860 to 1870, there was very little population growth recorded from within Chinatown.

However, the following interesting article was reported in the *Marysville Daily Appeal* on January 23, 1860:

> *CHINESS WEDDING*
> *Yesterday Judge Lucas "solemnized" another Chinese wedding. The happy pair, made one, was Ah Gee and Sing Gee. They were married in the presence of two "Melliken" men. L.T. Crane, County Recorder and officer Casad. After the ceremony the happy couple went their way rejoicing over the knot tied under a Yankee statute, and repaired to First street, where the nuptials were probably again celebrated according to the rites of the Celestials.*

One of the earliest Chinese births in Marysville was the son of Joe Bong and Yuet Woon Lew. Their first child, Joe Wing, was born in 1880 and followed by five more children, all born in the 1880s. The births in Marysville's Chinatown started to offset the Chinese who moved away or passed on. Another was the family of Hom Kun Foo and Lee Shee. Their first child, Hom Shoo Lin, was born in 1887, followed by four daughters and four sons.

Many of the children born between 1880 and 1910 had a difficult time with public education because they were not readily accepted by the school and the other students. It was difficult at best at that time, and they were picked on or in fights constantly. Because of this, many of the Chinese children during this period attended public school only for a very short time before dropping out.

In addition, many had to help their parents in the family business to sustain the business or work other jobs to support the family. Education was not considered a top priority. It was not until the family business was established that education became a priority and started to be stressed for the generations that followed.

These children were taught to succeed as a minority, and a good education is the foundation to get ahead in America. The parents felt that you must not merely be equal but also *better* than the general population.

Only very few of the second generation succeeded in education, but it wasn't until the third generation that the barriers for education began to weaken. The first Chinese child who attended public school was Joe Wing of the Joe Bong family, starting in the latter part of the 1880s.

Some of the children were taught that you can make a lot of money, but a good education is about more than that. You can lose all your money, but nobody can take away your education—even though public school officials often did not fully support the Chinese students in their pursuits.

Doreen Foo, a third generation from Marysville, remembered that in her junior year in high school, Mr. William Dawson, the principal of the Marysville High School, was visiting her class and asking the students what college they were planning to attend. Most of the students said University of California–Berkeley since, in those days, attendance there was free. However, Doreen responded that Stanford University was her choice. Mr. Dawson responded saying, "You'll never make it. You know why? Because first of all, you are a woman, and second, you're Chinese and they won't take you, because they will only take five hundred women and they don't like minorities."

After Doreen's senior year in high school, she attended the local community college for two years and applied to Stanford. She was accepted, graduating from Stanford in 1949.

Even though the Chinese formed a very small percentage of the total population in Marysville, they excelled in education. There were two who graduated from Marysville Union High School as valedictorians of their graduating class during the mid-1900s: Mabel Lim and Leonard Hom.

Chinese school was also important because the parents felt that due to high level of discrimination against the Chinese in the past, if their children did not get accepted in America, with their Chinese schooling, they could go to China for employment.

Edward Gee, grandson of Hom Kun Foo and Lee Shee, graduated from the University of California–Berkeley with a degree in civil engineering in 1934. Because of racial discrimination at that time in finding a job as an engineer, Edward decided to go to China to work. He worked as a civil engineer with the Kwang-Mei Railroad from 1934 to 1935 and taught civil engineering in southern China. With the onset of World War II, he returned to California in 1938 and was hired as a civil engineer at Mare Island Naval Shipyard. After the end of World War II, he began his career as the first licensed Chinese American real estate broker in San Francisco.

A typical weekday for Chinese children would be attending public school from 8:30 a.m. to 3:00 p.m. and Chinese school in the evening for three hours from 5:00 p.m. to 8:00 p.m. Chinese school continued on Saturday for three hours from 9:00 a.m. to noon. The program included reading, writing and reciting Chinese. The students were also taught to sing the Chinese national anthem. Any free time would be dedicated to studying or helping in the family business such as at a grocery store, laundry, restaurant and so on.

Many described their life during their adolescent period in Chinatown as difficult. But many felt that they developed an aptitude for hard work that carried over into their future years. Frank Kim, a native of Marysville and retired Superior Court judge in San Joaquin County, noted regarding the group of the thirty to forty Chinese friends who all lived in the Chinatown area from the 1920s to the 1940s, "We all went to college and not one of us went to prison."

The Chinese had a very high level of patriotism. Beginning in 1940s, all the eligible Chinese boys either enlisted or were drafted into the military service. All of them except John Yee returned to Marysville after serving. He was the only Chinese from Marysville killed in action during World War II. He was in the U.S. Army Air Corps on a bombing mission over China on a B-24, the Liberator. His family operated the Yee Hing laundry at 324 Second Street.

Many of those born from 1920 through the 1950s continued their education at the University of California–Berkeley, Stanford University, California State University–Sacramento and other universities and colleges. For those who served in the military, they could take advantage of the GI Bill.

Students in front of the Chinese School located at 22 C Street, 1940. *Courtesy Gene Sing Lim.*

This provided them an avenue to complete their education at a university or college.

After they completed their education, some returned to Marysville seeking employment but were not successful. Many found employment in the San Francisco, Oakland, San Jose or Sacramento metropolitan areas. The few who remained are scattered throughout Yuba and Sutter Counties, away from Chinatown. Many of them became medical doctors, elected officials, judges, attorneys, optometrists, pharmacists, engineers and more.

The following are some of the next generations from Marysville achieving the American Dream.

JOE WAUGH

Joe Waugh was one of first in the second generation to become very successful. He was born in 1886, the second son of Joe Bong and Lew Yuet Woon.

Along with his brother Joe Wing, Joe Waugh was among the first Chinese to attend public school in Marysville. Although the school principal, Walter Kynoch, strongly discouraged and at times prevented Chinese from attending classes, Joe Waugh was persistent and completed seventh grade before finally

Joe Waugh, 1922. *Courtesy Brenda Lee Wong.*

quitting because he was needed to help support his family financially. After Joe quit school, an elementary school teacher saw academic potential in Joe and continued to tutor him. When Principal Kynoch discovered that the teacher had been tutoring Joe, he fired the teacher.

During Joe's youth, he was the star southpaw pitcher of the first Chinese baseball team in Northern California. He played on both amateur and semipro teams. To support the family, he served as a houseboy for Hiram Johnson, a prominent lawyer, who was the twenty-third governor of California from 1911 to 1917 and was later elected a United States senator, serving thirty-eight years from 1917 to 1945 before passing.

While working for Hiram Johnson, Joe enjoyed reading and studying law books and case studies, and Johnson encouraged him. He mastered the English language quickly and spoke without a Chinese accent. He knew several dialects of Chinese and was able to help many Chinese immigrants throughout the state of California get their citizenship. Later, Hiram Johnson help Joe obtain his law degree, and Joe passed the bar exam. Joe did not want to get Johnson in any trouble, so he kept this information to himself.

After he started working for the various courts, Joe used the title of court interpreter instead of attorney of the courts. He was well known and in high demand by the county, state and federal courts throughout the state of California and at times traveled out of state to assist other courts. Because of his involvement with the courts, the opposing tongs were constantly trying to assassinate him. When he traveled to trials, he was accompanied by two Caucasian bodyguards. In some of his travels to court proceedings, he was fired at by tong henchmen.

Joe was an active member of the Marysville community and was a leader of the Hop Sing Tong Association. At times, he was the unofficial mayor of Marysville's Chinatown.

Because of his strong friendship with the local sheriff, Charles McCoy, Joe Waugh named his second daughter Bertha, after Charlie McCoy's wife.

TOM S. LUNG

Tom S. Lung, born in 1897, was part of the second generation in Marysville and third son of Hom Kung Foo and Lee Shee. During his teen years, he worked at the famous Western Hotel in Marysville as a busboy and bellhop for a short time. This work taught him at an early age what it is like to be humble and how unpredictable people can be, regardless of how well you treat them. He learned that there are good people and not so good people who treated Chinese very poorly. Because of the continual harassment, he decided to quit. He later took over managing the Tung Wo Company at 310 First Street, which his father, Hom Kun Foo, had started in the late 1800s.

Partnering with his brother Tom S. Suey, they opened businesses in Oroville, Stockton and San Francisco. In Marysville, he owned the Marysville Furniture Store and the Union Market with his other brothers. He also owned several gambling halls: Shanghai Company and the Quong Fat Company in Marysville, the White Front Company in Oroville and several others in Stockton. He was a major landlord in the center of Chinatown in San Francisco, owning one city block of two large apartment buildings on Stockton Street. He also operated a fireworks and firecracker business during celebrations for many years in Marysville and Yuba City until restrictive ordinances made the business unprofitable to continue.

Tom S. Lung, 1920s. *Courtesy Gordon Tom.*

He was a major contributor to the Chinese school at 226 First Street. At times, he was considered the unofficial mayor of Marysville's Chinatown in the 1940s and 1950s. He was well known not only in the Chinese community but also in the whole Marysville community.

ARTHUR TOM SR.

Arthur Tom Sr. (Chinese name Hom Hing) was a second generation born in 1904 at 310 First Street. He was the fifth and youngest son of Hom Kun Foo and Lee Shee and was the only son with a public school education. With his education and astuteness, he became very successful in the business community later in life. He had an excellent command of the English language and could speak without a Chinese accent, very important in the early 1900s. This allowed him to exit and return to America without any concern on the part of immigration officials.

In 1920, at the age of sixteen, he traveled to Toishan County in the Guangdong Province to attend the best herbal medicine school in the southern part of China. The school was operated by Chan Way Hing, the well-known doctor of herbal and traditional medicine. Years later, Arthur would repay his teacher by arranging the immigration of his son, Tom Y. Chan, to the America.

After being trained in herbal medicine, Arthur returned to the America in 1928 and partnered with Dr. W.S. Ling, an herbal medicine doctor in Oroville's Chinatown. Arthur acquired many of the herbal business practices from Dr. Ling, including the importance of advertising in the local newspaper, the use of testimonial letters from previous clients in his advertisement and developing contacts in San Francisco for his herbs. Dr. Ling had advertised and used testimonial letters as early as 1905 in the *Oroville Daily Register*, the local newspaper.

Arthur returned to Marysville in 1929 to practice herbal medicine at 310 First Street. Arthur recognized the importance of a business location to attract a broader clientele and started to look at other locations for his practice. He bought out an existing herbal business at 602 D Street and had a grand opening on January 9, 1933.

Arthur Tom Sr. in his reception room at his office at 602 D Street in 1933. *Authors' collections.*

The location of his practice being outside Chinatown and on the main business street in Marysville helped his business tremendously. It was an immediate success and became the largest Chinese herbal medicine office outside San Francisco. Most of his clients were white Americans who migrated to California from other rural areas of America where belief in herbal medicine was very strong.

Because he had an excellent command of both English and Chinese, he was the go-between for Chinese and the English-speaking community in Marysville. He was successful not only as a Chinese herb medicine doctor but also as a businessman. Among some of his business ventures were a chain of Savemor Department Stores, a Golden Eagle gas station, the National Hotel, the Marysville's Furniture Store and Union Market.

In his herbal business, he had the foresight to see the effects of world war on the importation of herbs to the United States. When World War II was in its infancy stages in China, he purchased great quantities of herbs in San Francisco, as much as the merchant would sell to him. After the war intensified, all trading with China ceased, and herbs were no longer being imported from China. Since Arthur had cornered the market on herbs earlier, he resold some of the herbs that he did not need back to the merchants in San Francisco for an extreme profit.

He was one of the four major contributors to the Chinese school located at 226 First Street in 1945. He was very active in the Suey Sing Tong Association in Marysville and a major contributor to the Chew Lun Family Association and the Tom Family Association in San Francisco.

One of his best friends was Dr. Leon Swift, the Yuba County Department of Health medical director.

Samuel Yee

Samuel Yee was born in 1909 in Marysville. He is the grandson of Joe Bong and Lew Yuet Woon. He was one of first Chinese to graduate from Marysville High School, in 1927. Because of his natural ability to speak before groups, he was the master of ceremonies at many events in Chinatown.

After high school, he opened a restaurant in Marysville's Chinatown and was very successful. However, he wanted to expand his restaurant business with a larger clientele. He moved to San Francisco and opened a restaurant at the 1939 Golden Gate International Exposition (World Fair)

Samuel Yee, JD, on the balcony of the Marysville Packard Library Building in 1927. *Courtesy Brenda Lee Wong.*

on Treasure Island in the San Francisco Bay. In the evening, he worked as the master of ceremonies at the well-known nightclub Forbidden City in San Francisco.

After the end of the exposition, he opened a restaurant in downtown San Francisco. This restaurant was located next to the University of California Hastings College of Law and was frequented by many of the law professors and staff from the college. Since he had an outgoing personality, he befriended them, and they advised him to go into law. After much persuasion, he enrolled in the University of California Hastings College of Law and graduated with a law degree (JD) in 1947.

He worked in private practice and also as a trial deputy city attorney for the City of San Francisco. He was appointed to the San Francisco Municipal Court by Governor Ronald Reagan. Among his credits was his admission in 1953 to practice before the Supreme Court of the United States. He became one of the foremost attorneys on immigration matters in California.

JACK KIM

In 1917, Jack Kim was one of the first Chinese Americans to be born in a hospital in Marysville. His home was 228 First Street in Marysville. Because of his small stature in grammar school, he was constantly being picked on. On one occasion, when he was with his brother, an older kid pushed and knocked him down. His brother beat the living daylights out of the kid, who never bothered Jack again.

After high school, Jack went into the service during World War II in the Seventieth Infantry Division, "Trailblazers," from 1944 to 1946. He fought as an infantryman on the front line in the Battle of the Bulge in Europe. It was the largest and most decisive battle and the turning point in World

Jack Kim, OD, at 228 First Street in 1947. *Courtesy Jack Kim.*

War II in Europe. Even though the Allied forces eventually won, there were massive casualties on both sides. Jack wasn't sure if he was going to live through the battle. This is something that he said he would never forget.

After discharge from the military, he returned to Marysville. He had a good singing voice and was the master of ceremonies for many events in Chinatown, including the Queen of Bomb Day dance in 1947.

Under the GI Bill, he attended and graduated with a Bachelor of Science degree from the University of California–Berkeley and received his optometry degree from the School of Optometry in 1951. He worked as an optometrist in San Francisco until his retirement in 1991.

BERTHA (BERT) WAUGH CHAN

Bertha Waugh, daughter of Joe Waugh, was born in 1924 in Marysville. Over the years, she owned a shoe store, sold real estate and was a licensed plumber (later owning a plumbing company). There are two ways to become a licensed plumber: train with another plumber for four years and pass an examination or own a plumbing business for four years and pass an examination.

When she was working as a bookkeeper for a plumbing company and the owner was going to Europe for several months, he asked Bertha to help him with the business. She agreed but only on the condition that she be allowed to buy into the business as a partner if the business was doing well when he returned. When the owner returned, the business was better than when he left for his trip. She became a partner in the business. She took plumbing classes and passed all the examinations with flying colors, becoming the first licensed female plumber in the state of California. However, aware of the physical limits of her strength, she stayed as the owner/plumbing contractor.

As a child, she was enthusiastic about taking ballet and tap dancing. This activity was the beginning of a lifelong passion for tap dancing. One of her instructors was Danny Daniels, who taught many actors and actresses how to tap dance. Some of her classmates included Nanette Fabray, Hal Linden, Marge Champion and Dick Van Dyke. After retiring from the plumbing/contracting business, she opened a tap dancing studio in Santa Monica. After managing the studio for forty years, she retired at ninety-two.

Bertha Waugh Chan
in 1940. *Courtesy Bertha
Waugh Chan.*

Her husband was George Chan. He was a set designer, production design and art director of movies and TV working for Twentieth Century Fox and Universal Studio. In 1970, George was nominated for an Academy Award for Best Art Direction for *Gaily, Gaily*. Although he did not win, Bertha mentioned that she enjoyed the gala celebration of the Academy Awards at the Beverly Hills Hilton Hotel with all the well-known people in the movie industry.

RUBY KIM TAPE

Ruby Kim Tape was the firstborn of Kim Wing and Woo Que, arriving in 1898 in Marysville. At age nineteen, she moved to San Francisco and attended a secretarial school. She was very active in San Francisco Chinatown community affairs, including the campaign to build the new Chinese hospital. She married Frank Tape of San Francisco. Frank Tape was the younger brother of Mamie

Tape, the plaintiff of *Tape v. Hurley*, the 1885 California Supreme Court case that held that the exclusion of a Chinese American student from public school based on ancestry was unlawful.

She later returned to Marysville and helped run the family store at 228 First Street. She continued her social work, such as building a playground in Marysville's Chinatown. In 1937, after Japan officially declared war on China, she became actively involved in war-related support work, such as raising funds for medical supplies and ambulances for the Chinese government.

After the Japanese attacked Pearl Harbor in 1941, Ruby wanted to serve her country more. She decided to join the U.S. Army, but because she was forty-four years old, her application was rejected at the Marysville recruiting office. She ignored the rejection and went directly to a U.S. Army field unit in San Francisco, took the physical exam and passed with flying colors. She became part of the Women's Army Auxiliary Corps (WAAC) in 1942. After her enlistment period was completed, she reenlisted for another six years.

She was assigned to the Military Intelligence Training Center at Camp Richie, Maryland, and provided support services for the training of interrogators, translators, order of battle researchers, photo interpreters

Ruby Kim Tape in the Women's Army Auxiliary Corps, 1944. *Courtesy Gene Sing Lim.*

and counterintelligence operators. In 1947, she was assigned to the Central Intelligence Group (the name later changed to Central Intelligence Agency, or CIA) in Washington, D.C.

She transferred to Japan and worked in the Supreme Commander of the Allied Powers organization and achieved the rank of Tec/Sergeant 5. She was awarded the American Campaign Medal, a World War II Victory Medal, an Army Commendation Ribbon, a Japan Occupation Ribbon and the Good Conduct Medal. After being discharged, she returned to California.

LEONARD HOM

Leonard Hom, PhD, was born in 1932 at 310 First Street. He is the grandson of Hom Kun Foo and Lee Shee. He attended Marysville Union High School and was valedictorian for the 1950 graduating class. He received his PhD in environmental engineering at the University of California–Berkeley. While at the California School of Public Health, he developed a water disinfection model that is still in use today. He started his teaching career at California State University–Sacramento in 1963 and retired as Professor Emeritus of

Leonard Hom, PhD. *Courtesy Leonard Hom.*

civil and environmental engineering in 1997. As Professor Emeritus, Leonard has served on the advisory board for the Environmental Engineering Program, advised graduate students on their theses and served as a consultant to public and private firms on environmental engineering issues. During the course of his teaching and research at CSUS, Leonard has presented research papers on environmental engineering issues at regional, national and international conferences that included Beijing, China, and Paris, France.

The Chinese American Pioneer Heritage Committee honored Leonard Hom with the Pioneer of the Year Award in 2019 at the Bok Kai Festival in Marysville.

BENJAMIN TOM

Benjamin Tom was born at 310 First Street. He was a grandson of Hom Kun Foo and Lee Shee. After Marysville High School, he graduated from the University of California–Berkeley in 1948. His working career was as a manager in the State of California Public Utility Commission. Benjamin was very active in the San Francisco Chinese community and was in the Chinese American Democratic Club, Chinese for

Benjamin Tom was elected to the San Francisco Board of Education in 1976. *Courtesy Gordon Tom.*

Affirmative Action, Chinese American Citizens Alliance and many other neighborhood groups. He was an active and vocal supporter of the integration of San Francisco's public school in the late 1960s and was elected to the San Francisco Board of Education in 1976. He was the the first Asian American to win a citywide election for public office in San Francisco and later became the president of the board. While in office, he championed bilingual education and the inclusion of ethnic studies in the San Francisco Public School System. He was the grand marshal of the 2006 Bok Kai Parade.

BRIAN TOM

Brian Tom, the fourth son of Arthur Tom Sr., was a graduate of UC Berkeley (BA) and received his law degree (JD) from the University of California–Davis School of Law. He was the founder of the Asian American Studies

Brian Tom, JD, displaying the Chinese medicine of his father, A.M. Tom Sr. *Authors' collections*.

(AAS) program at the University of California–Davis, one of the first AAS (June 1969) programs in the country. He was appointed coordinator of the program, and as the coordinator, he hired the first professors, designed the courses, set up the physical facilities of the program and taught classes. The AAS program at University of California–Davis was one of the first in the country to hire tenure track faculty members. He taught the first AAS class in the spring of 1969 and three of the first six classes offered in the program.

Later, as an attorney, he served as an administrative law judge for the State of California and was in private practice in San Francisco for more than twenty-five years. He is the founder and director of the Chinese American Museum of Northern California (CAMNC), which opened in 2007.

FRANK KIM

Frank Kim was a Superior Court judge in San Joaquin County. As one of the four Chinese American judges in California at that time, he was the second judge from Marysville.

His Chinese name is Jao Kim Hoong, and he was born in 1931 at 228 First Street, the Kim Wing Building. When he was less than a year old, his mother took him and his sister to China. When the war with Japan broke out, there wasn't sufficient funds for a third ticket back to the United States, so his mother just sent Frank and his sister back with friends. That was the last time he saw his mother. When he came back from China, he couldn't speak English and remembered being teased about not speaking English when he started public school.

He was raised by his uncle and aunt, and at the age of nine, he shined shoes on the corner of First and C Streets of Marysville. He would call out, "Want a shine mister, for a good shine, shine here, ten cents for a pair of shoes." He would go up and down the street after school, and on Saturdays, Sundays and summer vacations he would always made it a point to visit all the Chinese gambling halls in Chinatown. There were a lot of farm workers gambling, and he would always stand next to them with his shoeshine box. The winner would always give him lucky money. In Chinese, it is called Chung Chee, meaning "maybe you gave me good luck so here is a tip for you for bringing me good luck." Many times he would get a dollar or two from each place he visited. He would also receive tips from brothel workers in Chinatown.

He said that during the war years, the soldiers from Camp Beale were good tippers, and he would make up to twenty dollars per day shining shoes. That was a lot of shoes to shine at ten cents per shine. On weekends, he would be out at 9:30 a.m. in the morning and not get home until 5:00 p.m.

As he grew older, he started working during high school as a janitor at a law office in Marysville. He attended California State University–Sacramento and after graduating went into the military. He did not decide to become a lawyer until he was discharged from the military in 1954 after the Korean War.

Under the GI Bill, he attended University of California Hastings College of Law in San Francisco and earned his law degree (JD). He returned to Marysville, but the law firms would not hire him. He moved to Stockton, where he was hired as the first Asian American deputy district attorney in the San Joaquin County District Attorney's Office. After two years, he went into private practice.

In February 1971, California governor Ronald Reagan appointed him to fill a vacant judge position, and in 1979, Governor Jerry Brown appointed him as a Superior Court judge in San Joaquin County. He retired in 1991.

Frank Kim, JD, being sworn in as municipal court judge in 1971. *Courtesy Frank Kim.*

Being raised by a strict disciplinarian influenced his career as a judge on the bench. All the Chinese in his generation believe that you are responsible for your own actions—if you stole something from a store, you disgraced the family and you should be disciplined. As a result, he said, "You didn't see any Chinese kids in trouble in Marysville."

ELLA KIM WING

Ella Kim Wing, a third generation in Marysville, was born at 228 First Street. She was raised by her uncle Joe Lung Kim, who managed the gift shop on the ground floor at that address. She was the Queen of the Bok Kai Festival in 1947. After graduating high school, she completed secretarial school in San Francisco and worked at Jackson & Hertogs, a law office in Chinatown that specializes in immigration and naturalization cases. Over the course of her years with the law firm, she helped hundreds of families with their immigration process. She could not walk down Grant

Ella Kim Wing on the balcony of her home at 228 First Street. *Courtesy Gene Sing Lim.*

Avenue, the main thoroughfare in San Francisco's Chinatown, without being recognized by someone who was a former client of the law office.

In 2006, Ella had the honor of being the grand marshal of the Bok Kai Parade in Marysville, fifty-nine years after she had been crowned Bomb Day Queen in 1947.

ARTHUR TOM JR.

Arthur Tom Jr. and Lawrence Tom are third generation in Marysville, and both were born at 310 First Street.

Arthur, the first son of Arthur Tom Sr., graduated from the University of California–Berkeley and later received his MBA from San Jose State University. He returned to Marysville and managed a chain of department stores that his father started. He was very active in the Marysville and Yuba City communities. He was the foreman for the Sutter County Grand Jury, board member of the Yuba City-County Chamber of Commerce, president of the Yuba City Commercial Association and chairman of the Yuba City Retail Merchants Association, as well as was active in various other organizations.

He moved to San Jose and started a career as a commercial real estate broker. At the time Arthur entered the commercial real estate field, there were no Asian Americans practicing commercial real estate brokerage in Santa Clara County. He specialized in the sales of shopping centers and later office buildings and industrial building. He was a very successful commercial realtor in Santa Clara County. He also sold properties in several states outside California. He was the founder of the Chinese American Real Estate Association of Silicon Valley and was elected the founding president. Arthur felt that there was a need for an organization of this type to further advance the image of Chinese Americans in the real estate profession. The purpose of this association was to promote the social and economic well-being of members and further the professional image of Chinese Americans who are engaged in the field of real estate in the region.

Arthur has also been active in many community affairs in Santa Clara County. He has served as vice-president of the Chinese-American Chamber of Commerce in Santa Clara County, president of the Chinese American Citizens League, vice-president of the Organization of Chinese-Americans in Silicon Valley, chairman of Asian Heritage Week and a board member of

Arthur Tom and Lawrence Tom in front of their home in Chinatown at 310 First Street. *Authors' collections.*

the Chinese Historical Cultural Project and Asian Law Alliance. He has also served as a board member of the University of California–Berkeley Chinese Alumni and as its president in 1995–96.

LAWRENCE TOM

Lawrence (Larry) Tom, the second son of Arthur Tom, Sr., was a graduate of California State University–Sacramento (CSUS) with a degree in business administration. He also studied in the management program at the University of California–Davis (UCD).

Much of his work career has been in management in California state government. He was a career executive appointee (CEA) at the State of California Department of Transportation (CALTRANS). He held many management positions, including the department's chief of the Fiscal Systems Organization, and was the department's comptroller with a

Lawrence (Larry) Tom being presented with a Certificate of Appreciation for Outstanding Senior Volunteer 2015 in the Sacramento County Board of Supervisors meeting. *Authors' collections.*

statewide staff of six hundred employees. He was on the statewide California Fiscal & Personnel Management Information System (FPMIS) study task force that reported to the state legislature and was the chairman of a multi-departmental task force on the Feasibility Study for an Accounting System in 1972 for the newly created State Teale Data Center.

He was the founder and chairman of the State of California Fiscal Systems Council, president of the State of California Association of Managers and an officer and Most Valuable Member of the National Association of Accountants. He retired from state service in 2000.

In 2014, the Broadway Augmented virtual public art project in Sacramento, California—produced by the Sacramento Metropolitan Arts Commission, California State University–Sacramento and the Greater Broadway Partnership—recognized three prominent Chinese Americans in Sacramento. Lawrence Tom was one of the three recognized in the project. The other two were Jimmy Yee, a member of the Sacramento County Board of Supervisors, and Lena Fat, award-winning businesswoman of the Fat Family Restaurant Enterprise.

After Lawrence retired in 2000, he started volunteering. In 2015, he was recognized and awarded a Certificate of Appreciation by the Sacramento County Board of Supervisors for his services as the Outstanding Senior Volunteer in 2015.

PRENTICE TOM

Prentice Tom, MD, is the great-grandson of Hom Kun Foo and Lee Shee. He is the chief innovation officer and executive vice-president of medical affairs at Vituity. Since its start more than forty years ago, Vituity has grown beyond its California roots to include nearly four thousand doctors and clinicians working in acute care settings across the country. It is one of the largest operations of this type in the United States. He oversees the development and implementation of healthcare service solutions.

Prior to being appointed CIO, Dr. Tom served as chief medical officer, launching patient satisfaction initiatives and developing risk management and CMS programs. He also led two of Vituity's breakthrough initiatives, including Rapid Medical Evaluation® (RME) and emergency psychiatry. Additionally, he oversaw the development of Vituity's palliative care program, provided executive oversight for Vituity's administrative fellowship and created the practice's Clinical Education Department and CME programs.

Dr. Tom joined Vituity in 1993. He is a staff physician in the emergency department at Good Samaritan Hospital in San Jose, California. Before joining Vituity, he was a faculty member at Stanford University's Department of Emergency Medicine.

Dr. Tom has participated in numerous medical organizations, including the International Medical Corps (Bosnia) and Emergency International, where he served as long-term project coordinator for the China Project.

He holds a bachelor's degree in medical physics from the University of California–Berkeley and a medical degree from Harvard Medical School,

Prentice Tom, MD. *Courtesy Prentice Tom, MD.*

where he cofounded the Asian Health Organization. Dr. Tom completed his residency in emergency medicine at Johns Hopkins Hospital in Baltimore and was a Kaiser Fellow in health policy and management at the Massachusetts Institute of Technology (MIT).

GORDON TOM

Gordon Tom, born in 1941, is the grandson of Hom Kun Foo and Lee Shee. After graduating from Marysville High School, he served in the army and was stationed in Germany in 1959 with the Fourth Armored Division during the Cold War. After being discharged, he returned to Marysville to pursue many business ventures, including establishing the Golden T Automotive Company in 1966, and also to pursue a racing career. His automotive company manufactures off-road vehicles from the 1966 to 1972. His first vehicle, a GT Rhino, was sold to the movie star and singer Bing Crosby. In 1967, Gordon began off-road racing and was the first Chinese American in the sport in the United States. He competed in many off-road races, including the 1968 Mexican (Baja) 1000. This race

Gordon Tom in his Golden T Automotive Company office in 1966. *Courtesy Gordon Tom.*

was considered one of the most prestigious off-road races in the world, with participants coming from all over the world.

Gordon retired from off-road racing in 1976 and joined the various organizations for the preservation of Chinese history and traditions in Marysville. He later served as an officer in all of them and was the president of the Marysville Chinese Community Inc. from 2010 to 2013.

Gordon was the founder of the GT's Invitational Challenge Race in Marysville's Chinatown, an adult pedal car and push-cart race. He is a historian for Marysville's Chinatown, does tours of Chinatown and the Bok Kai Temple and also serves as a guest lecturer at the local college. He is one of the few Chinese who still resides in Marysville.

DAVID WING

David Wing's family owned two laundry businesses in Marysville. Laundry work requires heavy labor and working long hours. He graduated from Marysville High School in 1944 and was drafted into the army in 1945. He served at Camp Wolters Army Infantry Replacement Training Center.

Under the GI Bill, he attended the University of California–Berkeley. After graduating, he continued his education at the University of California Medical Center in San Francisco. He was a licensed bio-analyst in addition to earning the State Clinical Laboratory and the National ASCP licenses in 1957. He was the regional laboratory operations manager for Kaiser Permanente. He retired in 1991. He mentioned that if it wasn't for the GI Bill, he might have returned to Marysville to the laundry business.

David Wing, 1945. *Courtesy Gene Sing Lim*.

Deborah Jane Tom, MD, medical director for the Neonatology Unit, being recognized by *U.S. News Magazine* for 2018–19. *Courtesy Deborah Jane Tom, MD.*

DEBORAH JANE TOM

Deborah J. Tom is the great-granddaughter of Hom Kun Foo and Lee Shee. She graduated from the University of California–Davis. She completed her medical degree and pediatrics residency at Baylor College of Medicine in Houston, Texas, and her neonatology fellowship at Stanford University School of Medicine. She was an assistant professor at Baylor College of Medicine and had research funding from the National Institutes of Health grants. Dr. Tom is the medical director for the Phoenix Children's Hospital Neonatal Intensive Care Unit (NICU). Her organization is a Level IV NICU, delivering the highest level of complex neonatal care in the United States for very sick newborns. Her organization was recognized and ranked in the *U.S. News Magazine* "Top 50 Hospitals for Neonatology" for 2018–19.

KATIE FOO LIM

Katie Foo Lim, born in 1923, was a community leader and historian of Marysville's Chinatown. She and her husband, John, owned the Twin Cities Poultry business on C Street. They hosted many parties with visiting dignitaries and were called to represent the Chinese community at many cultural events. She was the driving force to reach out to Beale Air Force Base and to other parts of the community to have them participate in the annual Bok Kai Festival and make it an all-inclusive regional festival.

She was a special education instructional aide at the Marysville Elementary School and later taught cooking classes at Maysville High School.

Katie Lim with friend Jimmy Lim, 1940s. *Courtesy Gene Sing Lim.*

SHERMAN GEE

Sherman Gee, PhD, is a fourth generation and great-grandson of Hom Kun Foo and Lee Shee. He graduated from UC Berkeley and received his electrical engineering degree (MS) from the Massachusetts Institute of Technology (MIT) and PhD from Stanford University in 1965. He was an officer in the U.S. Air Force and later directed the communications networking applied research at the Office of Naval Research (ONR) in Arlington, Virginia. He was the U.S. representative in the North Atlantic Treaty Organization (NATO) on technology transfer in industrialized countries. In this capacity, he was the chairman on the steering committee of the international consortium consisting of eight European nations and NATO in developing and testing a new generation of internet for military application. He was also the conference chairman for the NATO Conference on technology transfer in industrialize countries in Estoril, Portugal, in 1977. The keynote speaker at this conference was U.S. Undersecretary of the Army Walter LaBerge. Among those participating were Dr. Joseph M.A.H. Luns, NATO secretary general; the NATO assistant secretary

Sherman Gee, PhD, with a letter dated January 31, 1979, from attendee NATO secretary general Dr. J.M.A.H. Luns thanking Sherman as chairman of the conference. *Courtesy Sherman Gee.*

general for scientific and environmental affairs; the Portuguese minister for industry and technology; and the chief judge of the U.S. Court of Customs and Patent Appeals.

These are some of the Chinese Americans who did not allow racial barriers to block their path to succeed and were able to excel in achieving the American Dream.

EPILOGUE

Chinatowns were established during the gold rush because the Chinese did not assimilate well into the general population when they first arrived in America. They came to a new land and did not understand the customs or language of their new country. They brought with them ideas, customs and traditions that differed from those already present in America at the time.

In addition, the anti-Chinese movement that started in the 1870s, coupled with the shortage of women, prevented the establishment of families, further slowing the assimilation by the next generations into the overall community.

In a Chinatown setting, the Chinese felt at ease with their own countrymen. They could understand the people, talk the language and eat the food they were familiar with back in China. In addition, many of the products and services they used and needed were not available outside Chinatowns.

The Chinese built more than thirty Chinatowns in Northern California during the gold rush period. Very little exists to remind us of their importance in their early settlement in California. Marysville's Chinatown is the last of the gold rush era still extant. Part of the forgotten history includes the roles Chinese Americans had in the development of modern Chinese history. Dr. Sun Yat-sen, the first president of the Republic of China, recognized the importance of the Chinese in America and visited the United States to learn more about democracy, raise funds, organize political opposition to the Ching Dynasty and recruit help for building a new China. He stayed in Marysville's Chinatown during his visits in the early 1900s. He recognized that Chinese Americans had the requisite skills—including in aviation, railroads and telecommunications—to help China develop into a modern nation.

Most Chinatowns across America are almost all gone, given the assimilation of the current generations into the community. Achieving the American Dream led to the demise of Chinatowns. As the Chinese assimilated into areas once forbidden to them, Chinatowns lost their inhabitants. Products that could only be purchased in a Chinatown in the past became readily available in most markets outside Chinatown.

With the exception of the largest cities in California such as San Francisco, Los Angeles and Oakland—where there are many recent and older immigrants arriving and housing available for the elders—Chinatowns are becoming a thing of the past in California.

Even Sacramento's Chinatown, once quite large, is near the end of its existence. It was referred to as an "Administrative Chinatown" in the book *150 Years of the Chinese Presence in California, 1848–2001*. The only things remaining are several tong association buildings, the Chinese Confucius Church Building and the Dr. Sun Yat-sen Memorial Hall. There are no Chinese-owned retail establishments in the Sacramento Chinatown Mall.

The Sacramento Chinatown Mall was the site of a Chinese Culture Fair that was held for several years in September for an expression of Chinese culture and the recognition of the journey and contribution of the Chinese immigrants to America. That ended in 2013 due to the lack of support and continuing interest.

Marysville's Chinatown was once a thriving place but has been through its glory days. Prior to the 1940s, certain parts of Marysville were off limits to the Chinese. Beginning in 1940s, the Chinese slowly started to integrate to the northern and eastern parts of Marysville. In the past, the city realtors would not sell to Chinese (de facto housing practices) or were very blunt about it, telling the Chinese, "I can't sell to you because you are Chinese."

The Chinese pioneers who settles in Marysville's Chinatown were from the Sze Yup counties. The people from these counties are confident, adventurous and refuse to give up. Although very few Chinese reside in Marysville's Chinatown today, the subsequent generations kept it alive because of the spirit of the Chinese pioneers. They understood the importance of maintaining the history for future generations.

The center of Chinatown was at First and C Streets. The beginning of C Street starts at the levee and was an unpaved dead-end street to First Street. At the foot of the levee was a swing set, slide, wading pond and picnic tables. This area was considered the park and playground in Chinatown and was used on a regular basis by the children in Chinatown for all their outdoor activities. It was also used as gathering place for outdoor events by the Chinese community.

Facing the playground area, at 22 C Street, was the location of the second Chinese school, which was opened between 1935 and 1945 before moving to the last location at 226 First Street. Next door to the Chinese school was the Chinese Presbyterian Mission Church, located at 24 C Street. The mission church began in 1880 and operated at several locations in Chinatown before moving in 1920 to the 24 C Street location. It was a very active mission and played an important part in the lives of the Chinese community. It provided many organized activities and had a small library for the children. In 1924, the mission organized the Chinese Boy Scout Troop No. 5. Although the scoutmaster was non-Chinese, the assistant scoutmaster was. The local newspapers reported that the program

Chinese teenagers playing football in the unpaved area of C Street. Mary Ong is holding the football for Jack Kim, circa the 1940s. *Courtesy Bing Ong.*

Left: Students with missionaries in front of the Chinatown's Presbyterian Chinese Mission, 1942. Mrs. Hattie Robinson is the missionary in front. *Courtesy Gene Sing Lim.*

Below: Chinatown's baseball team in the 1920s. *Courtesy Brenda Lee Wong.*

was "a stirring Americanization meeting" with elections, citizenship talks and playing of American games. The mission in the 1920s also sponsored the Celestial Boys' Club, a baseball team and a basketball team for the Chinese children.

The mission also played an important role with the women in Chinatown. The missionaries taught English as part of their program. One important project of the mission during the war in China in 1939 was assisting the women's division of the Marysville Chinese War Relief effort. A group of Chinatown's women sewed and prepared a huge supply of bandages for the war effort. All the work was completed at the Chinese Presbyterian Mission Church by the local Chinese women. Participating in this effort were Mrs. Gar Yee, Mrs. Lung Kim, Mrs. Yee Kay, Mrs. Wong Guey, Mrs. Chin Yuk, Mrs. Lim Foo, Mrs. Suey Tom, Mrs. A.M. Tom and Mrs. Ong Tall.

The mission operated at 24 C Street for four decades until the 1960s and closed due to lack of attendance as the Chinese families moved out of the Chinatown area.

As the second generation became well established, education was stressed for the subsequent generations. The Chinese were also taught

Marysville's Chinese women sewing bandages for the 1939 war relief effort in China. *Authors' collections.*

that you do not do anything that will disgrace the family or the Chinese community. The most active generation of Chinese in Marysville were the group born during the 1920–40 period. This group lived through the Great Depression in the 1930s and then the impact of World War II and the Korean War.

This group assimilated well into the general population, and many have succeeded in spite of the discrimination and hardships they encountered. They managed to fulfill a significant portion of the American Dream that their parents had hoped for, while, at the same time, remaining true to their heritage and Marysville's Chinatown.

Since all the Chinese lived in Chinatown prior to the 1950s, the children grew up together and formed a very close-knit group. In the 1940s, the group formed a marching band. All the funding for the band was raised by the students. The instruments were donated or purchased from the fundraising events. The uniforms were designed by Jimmy Lim, a member of the group, and sewn by all the girls in the band with the help and guidance of the high school economics teacher. Marching and drill instructions were provided by several members who were already members

The marching band formed by the Chinese youth in Chinatown in 1940s. *Authors' collections.*

of the high school band. It was a total effort by the Chinese community and provided an enormous amount of satisfaction and camaraderie for all the young people in Chinatown.

This group participated in the activities at the Chinese Presbyterian Mission Church and the Chinese school, and most attended college. Although none of them lived in Marysville anymore, they still kept close contact with one another.

According to Gene Sing Lim, the group started meeting in the late 1950s for a reunion for the prior inhabitants of Marysville's Chinatown. Gene said that the reason they all keep coming back is because of their lifelong friendships. "We all grew up together in the neighborhood when it was really a neighborhood, and all of our houses were on and near First and C Streets."

The first reunions were in Marysville; however, several of the subsequent ones were held either in the San Francisco Bay Area or Sacramento. There were very few of that generation remaining in Marysville, as most had moved to the metropolitan areas for education and employment.

The seventh Marysville's Chinatown reunion was being planned in 2002; however, the reunion never took place because the group was getting older, some had difficulty in traveling and some had passed on.

Marysville's Chinatown is unique from other Chinatowns. The Chinese pioneers passed on to their children the importance of maintaining its heritage. Each year, many of the elders would return to enjoy the Bok Kai celebration and worship at the temple, just as they had done in the past.

The Fourth Marysville's Chinatown Reunion, held in San Mateo in May 1991. *Courtesy May Tom Lum.*

The planning meeting for the seventh Marysville's Chinatown reunion in March 2002 in San Jose. *Authors' collections.*

The grand opening of the Chinese American Museum of Northern California in 2007 at 232 First Street started a revival of Marysville's Chinatown. This was an ideal location for the museum, being in the center of Chinatown and the location where the Chinese have fired the bombs for Bomb Day for more than 150 years. The museum's objective was to preserve and interpret the forgotten history of the Chinese in America. The key exhibit in the museum is *Chinese American History in 10 Easy Steps*. Many of the visitors to the museum remarked that this exhibit was the highlight of their visit here because it brought together the difficult journey of the Chinese to America from the past to the present.

The Chinese school building at 226 First Street has recently been converted to a museum and opened in 2018. This museum is a collection of Marysville Chinese artifacts. Another museum is being created in the Council Chamber at the Bok Kai Temple. These are all managed and operated by the descendants of the original Chinese pioneers—Gordon Tom of the Hom Kun Foo family and Ric Lim of the Joe Bong family, both still residing in Marysville.

Continuing efforts to maintain the Bok Kai Temple and the museums will ensure learning centers for future generations to gain an appreciation and understanding of the struggles and achievements of the Chinese pioneers.

Marysville's Chinatown is now but a remnant of its once great strength in numbers, but it has maintained itself nevertheless throughout the years as an integral part of Marysville that has brought much credit to the city. Much of this quality is being portrayed in the series of events that form the Bok Kai Festival celebration. More recently, several conferences on Chinese history have been held in Marysville's Chinatown during the Bok Kai celebration to stimulate interest in preserving Chinese American history.

In 2019, the Marysville's Chinese brought a new wealth of activities and a new height of interest to the observance, going beyond the normal capacity of their strength to give the unique observance a quality and hue that set it apart more than ever in the United States.

The Chinese American Pioneer Heritage Committee worked to increase knowledge of the historic Marysville Chinatown, once the second largest in the United States, and to honor Chinese American role in building California—especially the railroads, roads, wineries, mines, delta levees, water and irrigation systems and agricultural farmlands. The conference also honored the 150th anniversary of the Golden Spike, the completion of the Transcontinental Railroad.

In conjunction with the Bok Kai Parade and Festival, the program included educational and cultural events. It also included a Chinese American film festival that featured a spectrum of documentaries of Chinese American history, pioneers and community life, as well as workshops on the history of the Chinese and Asian immigrant experience and the impact of the Chinese Exclusion Act.

Marysville's Chinatown still survives because the descendants of the first pioneers remain and keep their traditions alive with the Bok Kai Festival. They understand that if their Chinatown disappears, the last link to the beginning of Chinese history in America will be lost forever.

Marysville is not similar to other Gold Country towns, where the only evidence remaining of the pioneering work of the early Chinese in those towns is in a small display at a local museum or in artifacts displayed in an antique store. Marysville's Chinatown will survive, even though there are only two Chinese-owned business remaining in Chinatown. It still has an active temple that is used for worship, two Chinese museums, the Hop Sing Tong Association, the Marysville Chinese Community Inc. organization and the traditional Chinese festivals. Chinatown will not be forgotten because the spirit of the pioneers laid the foundation for future generations to succeed. The words of the pioneers can be heard: "Never surrender."

So, as the Yee Yuet Yee date (the second day of the second month on the lunar calendar) approaches, the Marysville Chinese community unpacks the "Lung" (dragon), makes the bombs for Bomb Day, sweeps out the temple and prepares to celebrate another year in Old Gold Mountain.

LIST OF MARYSVILLE CHINATOWN BUSINESSES IN 1913

From the International Chinese Business Directory for the Year 1913

MARYSVILLE CHINATOWN BUSINESSES

First Street between A and D Streets

76 First Street Chong Wing, General Merchandise
111 First Street Quong Tuck Lung, General Merchandise
215 First Street Kim Chong Chew Kee, Groceries
215 First Street Leung Kee & Company, General Merchandise
218 First Street Lim Got & Company, General Merchandise
216 First Street Lun Hing & Company, General Merchandise
220 First Street Lin Kee & Company, General Merchandise
222 First Street Wing Yuen & Company, General Merchandise
223 First Street Yuen Wah & Company, General Merchandise
225 First Street Yut Loy & Company, General Merchandise
226 First Street Hang Lung & Company, General Merchandise
232 First Street Quong Hop Ket kee, Drugs and Merchandise
301 First Street Wing On & Company, Tobacco

302 First Street Wo Yuen, General Merchandise
306 First Street Duck Chong, General Merchandise
308 First Street Quong Hong On & Company, General Merchandise
310 First Street Chong Wo & Company, Chinese Merchandise
314 First Street Sue Sing Lung, General Merchandise
322 First Street Kwong Sing, General Merchandise

Second Street between C and D Streets

Leon Hop & Company, Chinese Fancy Goods

C Street between the Levee and Third Street

10 C Street Bin Chin Tie Kee, General Merchandise
10 C Street Yut Hing Low, Restaurant
6 C Street Chung Gee Tong, Society
20 C Street Quong Hop, Drugs and Merchandise
25 C Street Yee Hing & Company, Tobacco
27 C Street Ying Yuen & Company, General Merchandise
101½ C Street Hop Sing Tong Society
102 C Street Chong Wo, General Merchandise
103 C Street Wing Tai Lung & Company, General Merchandise
107½ C Street Quong Chong & Company, General Merchandise
109 C Street San Yuen Sang & Company, Cigars
109 C Street Yuen Sang & Company, Cigar Manufacturers
113 C Street Yen King Lum, Restaurant
113 C Street Woy Sen Low, Restaurant
115 C Street Hong Wo Tong & Company, Drugs
229 C Street Kim Shang, Laundry
229 C Street Yee Wing & Company, Laundry

Other Streets

101 Third Street Wy Lung, General Merchandise
119 Ninth Street Hong wo Tai & Company, General Merchandise
304 E Street Tai Sing & Company, Laundry

APPENDIX A

Others with PO Box

PO Box 386 Hong Wo & Company, General Merchandise
PO Box 284 Sue Chong, General Merchandise

Others No Address

Congregational Chinese Mission
Born Kee, Tobacco
Chung Hwa National Association
Quong Hop Lung, General Merchandise
Quong Wa Sing, General Merchandise
Sam Sing, Laundry
San Lee Hong Kee & Company, General Merchandise

CHINESE AMERICAN HISTORY IN
10 EASY STEPS

Exhibit displayed at the Chinese American Museum of Northern California.

1. CHINA, 1800s

Still the Middle Kingdom

In the middle of the nineteenth century, when the Chinese first started immigrating to America, China was among the richest countries in the world. It was a leader in agricultural technology, medicine, the culinary arts and the production of consumer products. In 1850, China produced 33% of the world's gross domestic product.

Many of America's early leaders, among them Benjamin Franklin and Thomas Jefferson, admired the achievements of the Chinese civilization. In particular, they thought the Chinese examination system, a system that was open to everyone and rewarded merit, was worthy of emulation.

Chinese tea was almost universally enjoyed by the founding fathers and almost all used china (porcelain) and silk in their households.

Though China was still wealthy at that time, monumental change was rapidly developing.

For centuries, trade between the West and China was overland along the Silk Road. The Europeans were never happy about this state of affairs. The road was long, dangerous and expensive due to the high tariffs imposed on trade by tribal leaders along the Silk Road.

A new way had to be found to more directly secure the riches of the "Indies" (the lands that lay east of the Indus River, China being the most important). The European "age of exploration" was set off by a search for a sea route to the Indies.

2. THE CHINA TRADE: ACCUMULATING CAPITAL IN A CAPITALIST AGE

The Opium War: The Beginning of the End for the Qing Dynasty

The Portuguese were the first Europeans to establish trade relations by sea with China when Father Francis Xavier built a trading post at Shangchuan Island, Taishan (Toishan) County, Guangdong Province, in 1551 six years before they settled in Macao. Taishan County would later play a large role in Chinese American history.

During the 17th and most of the 18th century, trade with the West developed very slowly as China had little interest in products offered by the Europeans. In 1757, in order to maintain control over the trade with Europeans, China restricted trade with the West to Canton (Guangzhou).

England soon overtook Portugal as China's largest European trading partner. The balance of trade always favored China as English goods had a limited market in China. England made up their trade deficit with silver. This presented England with a major economic problem as the Age of Capitalism was beginning and capital was critical for development into a capitalist country.

In order to balance trade and accumulate capital, England entered the illicit drug trade. Building huge opium plantations in their colony of India, England started selling large quantities of opium to China. In 1800, England shipped 850,000 lbs. of opium to China; by 1879, shipments totaled 13,400,000 lbs. England had become the largest drug dealer in the world.

The United States also entered the drug trade with opium from Turkey. America faced the same problem as England. It had little to sell the Chinese. The major items that Americans had for sale to China were silver, ginseng roots, furs and sandalwood. China traders in New England hired local root diggers to forage for ginseng. Fur pelts were traded in the frontier West. But the major source of pelts was seals and otters nesting on the islands located off the tip of South America. Millions of seals were killed on the sea route to China to the point of extinction. In 1796, the *Neptune* sailed out of New Haven, slaughtered 80,000 seals in the South Pacific, and returned with a profit of $220,000, an enormous sum in those days.

But the real money was in drugs. The list of New England families that made their fortunes in opium included the following: Russell, Perkins, Delano, Cabot, Coolidge, Forbes, Low and Green.

The drug dealers became major capitalists by expanding into banking, insurance and international finance. Profits from the opium trade build the beautiful residences of Salem, Massachusetts, and helped finance the Union Pacific Railway.

The use of opium created major domestic problems for the Chinese that permeated every aspect of society. In addition, the balance of trade was now in favor of the Westerners as silver to pay for the opium was being drained from the Chinese economy at an alarming rate.

The emperor made one last attempt to control the opium trade. In 1839 he appointed Lin Zexu High Commissioner to eradicate the opium curse. Commissioner Lin wasted no time in formulating a plan. Opium had to be controlled at the source. First he wrote to Queen Victoria:

> *The Way of Heaven is fairness to all. It does not suffer us to harm others in order to benefit ourselves.....Suppose there were people from another country who carried opium for sale to England and seduced your people into buying and smoking it; certainly you would deeply hate it and be bitterly aroused...*
> —*Commissioner Lin, 1839*

Commissioner Lin then asked the queen to stop the manufacture of opium in India and destroy all the opium that had already been produced. He also confiscated and burned all the opium in Guangzhou.

Her majesty's response was swift and brutal. She sent warships to the Chinese coast and bombarded the Chinese into submission. Faced with an enemy with vastly superior firepower and suffering horrendous casualties, the emperor capitulated. The surrender terms were harsh: 1. Open five ports, including Canton and Shanghai, to further develop the opium market. 2. Grant extraterritoriality to all British citizens. 3. Cede Hong Kong to the British.

The defeat of the Chinese in the First Opium War opened the floodgates of hell into China as the evil drug soon devastated the country. Joining the British in exploiting China's weakness were all the European powers and America. The Western countries would continue selling opium to the Chinese well into the 20th century, consigning millions to wasted and destructive lives.

Within England, many saw that opium trade was immoral, but they were in the clear minority:

> I am in dread of the judgment of God upon England for our national iniquity towards China.
>
> —William Gladstone, 1842

The opium dealers justified their sale of opium as a kindness to the Chinese:

> The use of opium is not a curse, but a comfort and benefit to the hard-working Chinese.
>
> —1858 press release from the British firm of Jardine, Matheson & Company

Unable to protect the Chinese people, the Qing Dynasty was losing the Mandate of Heaven.

3. THE CANTONESE: THE MOUNTAIN IS HIGH AND THE EMPEROR IS FAR AWAY

The Siyi (Sze yup) Counties: A Special Place

Canton (Guangzhou) is the capital of Guangdong Province, the home of the Cantonese people.

From 1760 to 1843 Canton was the only port open to trade with the West. Being the entry point for commercial intercourse with the West would have tremendous impact on this province. As trade developed, Guangdong began to develop a rudimentary market economy. A growing infrastructure developed to handle foreign trade, including the construction of new transportation facilities and development of local industries to meet export demands. Traditionally Guangdong was always considered a rich province because of its productive farmlands, abundant rainfall, an extensive river transportation system, a history of commercial activity and a reputation for academic achievement. With a monopoly on trade with the West, Guangdong further secured its status as a rich province. That status continues to this day. Guangdong has the highest GDP of any province in China.

The Cantonese are the most independent of all the Chinese. They are the natural rebels of China. "The mountain is high, and the emperor is far away," the Cantonese like to say. It is a reminder that the central authority must travel a long and difficult road to reach Guangdong. The Cantonese think of themselves as the true Chinese, unlike the northerners that have been tainted by too close a contact with the barbarians that invaded from beyond the Great Wall. For the Cantonese, unlike the rest of China that considers the Yangtze River the dividing line, everything north of Guangzhou is "the North."

Both Chinese and Western observers have noticed the special characteristics of the Cantonese.

> *Cantonese are worldly men of affairs, shrewd bargainers, knowledgeable in technology, frank in criticism, oriented to defending their own interest. They are quick, lively, and clever in catching on to new skills...*
>
> *−Vogel, 1969*

The Cantonese compared to people in other parts of China were traditionally regarded as adventurous, progressive and combative people. These characteristics would prove very helpful as China responded to the new challenges from the West.

Located 50 miles from Guangzhou in the western part of the Pearl River Delta, Siyi ("Four Counties")—composed of Toishan (Taishan), Sunwui, Enping and Kaiping (Hoiping)—played a leading role in the emigration of the Chinese to America. Toishan was and is the most important county among the four with the largest population and land area, and by far the longest seacoast.

The Siyi counties are a beautiful part of Guangdong with rich river valleys and rolling hills that in places erupt into rugged mountains. The area is blessed with rich soil that supports two or three crops of rice a year. It is famous for the variety of fruits and vegetables grown there.

These four counties are the home counties of 80 percent of the pre-1965 Chinese emigrants to America. More than half came from Toishan alone. In China, Toishan is called the "Home of the Overseas Chinese."

All the characteristics of the Cantonese people apply to the people from the Siyi counties, perhaps to even a more exaggerated degree. The one characteristic that best defines the Siyi people is their stubbornness. They refuse to give up even when the situation appears hopeless.

They are heirs to a rich history of resistance. When the Mongols invaded China in 1271, they swept in from the north and forced the ruling Song Dynasty south. The Song Dynasty armies fought bravely, but they were no match for the Mongol hordes. By the end of the decade, the imperial court had retreated to Siyi. It was in Siyi that the Song Dynasty would make its last stand.

In 1279, the Song naval forces suffered a devastating defeat at the Battle of Yamen near Sze Yup. The end was near. Vowing never to surrender to the barbarians, the prime minister of the Song Dynasty, Lu Xiofu, strapped the Song boy emperor to his back and leaped into the South China Sea near a seaport on the Toishan Sunwui county line.

With the death of the emperor, the Song forces, composed of many high-ranking officials and military officers, disbanded and settled in Toishan, Sunwui and the surrounding counties. The presence of the remnants of the Song Dynasty imperial court would have a strong influence on Siyi. Even today, many families with the surname Chew, Jew and Jue claim descent from the Song royal line.

Siyi people have never forgotten the loyalty of Lu Xiofu, and a memorial has been erected to him in the western part of Toishan. "Never give up" became part of the history of the Siyi people.

4. Emigration: An Important Step in China's Modernization

Many historians have focused on economic hardship as the only cause of Chinese emigration to America. The reasons espoused have been reduced to a simplistic formula of "fighting, flood, and famine." The fighting part of the formula cites the Taiping Rebellion, but as can be seen by the map to the right, the Rebellion, though it was led by a Cantonese, never reached Guangdong. In addition, the Taiping Rebellion started after the Chinese started emigrating to America.

Flooding and famine were constants in a pre-modern China that affected every region of the country. The Pearl River Delta was able to weather the effects of these natural calamities better than many other parts of the country because it was more developed. Rather than being the poorest province, Guangdong was among the richest. The almost one century when Canton was the only open port for trade with the West affected the Pearl River Delta economy in a profound way. Trade created wealth. In 1850, the richest man in the world was a Cantonese merchant named Howqua, who made his fortune in international trade. His fortune was so immense he invested in projects in England and the United States.

As the filter through which all Western trade had to pass, Canton along with the surrounding Pearl River Delta soon surpassed the other provinces that had no access to international markets. The reliance on a subsistence agriculture economy was no longer necessary. Now food, primarily rice and other grains, was being brought in from Southeast Asia to feed the people.

A forgotten reason for emigration had its roots in the political history of Guangdong. In 1644, the Manchus invaded from the north, breached the Great Wall and occupied Beijing. The Ming Dynasty court fled south. Capturing the capital did not mean the end of the Ming. Just as when the Mongols invaded, the conquest would take years. The Qing warriors forced the Ming south. Fighting would continue for another decade and a half as the new Qing Dynasty consolidated its power.

As the southernmost province, Guangdong once again played host to the victims of a barbarian attack from the north. In the early 1650s the Ming Emperor, Yongli, established his capital at Zhaoqing in the Pearl River Delta. As the Qing forces advanced, he fled to Guangxi. But he left many loyal forces in Guangdong. A resistance movement by the loyalists of the Ming grew. They built a fortress in the south of Toishan at Wencun where they fought off the Manchu armies for years. Finally in 1659, Wencun was defeated, the last stronghold of the Ming Dynasty.

The Qing Dynasty, seeking revenge against the Cantonese for their fierce resistance, instituted polices to prevent a rebellion. Much of the resistance to the Qing had been supported by the Cantonese who had traveled abroad to places like Taiwan, the Philippines and Southeast Asia. To break this connection, the Qing decreed that any area within 16 miles of the coastline was a "dead zone." Anyone caught in the dead zone would be summarily executed. Toishan, with one of the longest coastline of any country in Guangdong, was the most heavily affected.

In addition to creating a dead zone, the Qing also outlawed emigration on the penalty of death and requested that foreign governments repatriate those that had gone abroad. All emigrants were treated by the Qing as traitors or potential traitors. This law would remain in effect until 1894 when it was finally repealed.

Almost from the time the Manchus completed their conquest, the Cantonese started a resistance movement. The Cantonese never forgot the lesson taught by Minister Lu Xiufu: "Never give up."

When the British started the Opium War and invaded Guangdong the Cantonese did not wait for the Manchus to defend them. Rather, they organized local militias to fight. In San Yuan Li, the local militia routed the English in one of the few battles the Chinese won. From this battle, the Cantonese developed a strong hatred for the British:

> *You have killed and injured our common people in many villages, and seriously hurt the universal harmony....This is properly a time when Heaven is angered and mankind is resentful...*
> *—Cantonese placard, 1841*

The hatred for the English was so strong that the British, after winning the Opium War, rather than try to expand their presence in Guangzhou, moved north to the friendlier city of Shanghai.

At the same time, the Cantonese understood that in order to defend China, they had to modernize their society by using technology from the West. The Cantonese had tasted directly how destructive Western technology could be if used for evil purposes. They felt that by combining Western technology with Chinese culture, they could produce a more harmonious society. It is a dream they are still pursuing today.

Canton had always been one of the intellectual and academic centers of China. Starting with the Opium War, the students, scholars and mandarins of Canton would study and debate how to modernize China. They were particular interested in the relatively new country of the United States, a country that rebelled against England and formed a democracy. Unlike the hated British, the Chinese had always felt that the Americans were a more fair and honest people.

Economic opportunity, overthrowing the Qing, modernizing China and studying the political system of democracy—all were important themes in examining the larger narrative of Chinese emigration to America.

For the Cantonese, these were not mere abstract concepts to be discussed over a cup of rice wine. Almost from the day the first Cantonese set foot on American soil, they formed secret societies (Tongs or Triads). These Tongs were established for the very purpose of destroying the Qing Dynasty. "Fan Qing, Fu Ming" ("Overthrow the Qing, Restore the Ming") was their rallying cry. Every member of a tong was sworn to support this cause.

About 90% of the Chinese that emigrated to America joined a Tong. While it is difficult to estimate how many of the Chinese immigrants came here for political purposes, it would be hard to deny that overthrowing the tyrannical Qing Dynasty played a large role in motivating the Chinese to come to a nation that was

"…conceived in liberty and dedicated to the proposition that all men were created equal."

5. GLOBALIZATION BEGINS: A WORLDWIDE RUSH FOR GOLD

The Gold Rush in California marks the beginning of globalization. For the first time in human history, transportation and communications had advanced to such a state that people from all over the world could come to one location to work and compete with one another. The immensity of the California gold discovery provided the irresistible incentive to come.

From Europe came the British, Spanish and French. Chileans and Peruvians arrived from South America. Australians joined the Gold Rush. Hawaiians took part. And of course, Americans from the eastern part of the United States as well as Sonorans from Mexico came. Adventurers from the largest continent of all, Asia, also joined the gold rush.

A number of Asian countries could have sent adventurers. Japan was the closest to the West Coast of America. Korea was a little farther away to the north of Japan. China lay in between those two countries and the countries of Thailand, Philippines, Burma, Malaysia and Indonesia. India was just a little farther west.

Yet except for the citizens of one country, China, no Asians from any country in Asia joined in the California Gold Rush. More interesting still is that of the many regions of China, only the citizens of one province, Guangdong, made the trip across the Pacific. It would be up to the Cantonese, with their tradition of adventure and rebellion, to represent Asia in the greatest Gold Rush in history.

In the mid-19th century, the Western powers were completing their domination of the world. Great Britain, the Netherlands, France, Spain and later even the United States were colonizing the less developed countries of Asia and Africa. Mystical powers were ascribed to the mighty Westerners. Militarily, economically and culturally, the Western powers had no rivals. As a result, in that era, no group of people from a less developed country had ever freely migrated to a Western country.

But the California Gold Rush was unique. Not only for the amount of the gold that had been discovered but also because much like the Internet today, the gold was free. When gold was discovered, California was in transition from Mexican rule to becoming a state of the United States. Land ownership was uncertain and in flux. A governmental structure had not been set up to enforce property rights. Gold was literally "free for the taking."

When word came from across the Pacific that gold had been discovered, the Cantonese knew exactly what that meant. Ever since China lost the Opium War, the Cantonese were looking for just such an event. It represented an opportunity to further their hopes to overthrow the Qing Dynasty. The gold meant money to finance a revolution; travel to a western country would help the modernization of China.

Once in California, the Chinese found a surprisingly egalitarian society. California was almost unsettled at the beginning of the gold rush so everyone that found their way there was a pioneer with the pioneer's spirit of treating everyone by what they could contribute to building a new society.

In the gold fields, the Chinese quickly saw that they could compete with the Westerners. For a start, they had superior food and medicine. Boiling water for the tea they drank kept them much healthier than the Western miners. Where the Western miners seldom mined in partnerships of more than two or three, the Chinese, through clan or Tong affiliations, could form partnerships of twenty or thirty. These large partnerships allowed the Chinese to profitably mine claims that the individual Western miners had given up on. By using their skills in the control of water, the Chinese built wing dams that diverted the course of the streams and rivers where the gold was. Guangdong had a silver mining industry, and a number of Cantonese silver miners joined the gold rush and used their expertise to extract gold from the hills.

The opportunity that the Cantonese had waited more than two hundred years for had finally arrived. The Gold Rush gave the Cantonese the chance to accumulate ideas and capital to further their political ambitions. The long process to "overthrow the Qing" had begun.

6. CHINESE PIONEERS IN AMERICA

The Chinese quickly established themselves in the Gold Country, building Chinatowns in all the gold centers in the Sierra foothills and later expanding their reach into the Trinity Mountains in Weaverville. Free to travel and settle in any part of the state, they took full advantage of their newfound freedom. Compared to their home country, where they were bound by tradition and unchanging land ownership, where families had lived in the same location for hundreds of years, they encountered a land that was unsettled and unpopulated, open to being developed by anyone that had the ability and time. It was like entering a land of unlimited possibilities.

In the first two decades of living in California, the Chinese built over 30 Chinatowns. In those days, more than 90% of the Chinese lived in these small-town Chinatowns. The San Francisco Chinatown would not attain its prominence until later.

The Chinese introduced Buddhism and Taoism to North America. In every Chinatown they built a temple where their gods could be worshiped, at the same time reminding European Americans that there are many gods in this world.

The spread of Chinese culture in California grew as the new Chinese pioneers opened Chop Suey or "fusion" restaurants featuring Chinese and American dishes throughout the state. Food was the first contact that many European Americans had to Asian culture.

They made a place for themselves in the California economy. They started the fishing industry and did most of the work to start the agricultural industry. In urban occupations, cigar making, woolen mills, salmon packing, boot making and domestic work, they either were a major presence or dominated those industries. Railroad work was another area in which they excelled. During this period the Chinese constituted 25% of the total California workforce.

For a time, the Chinese thought they had found the Promised Land as they were no longer oppressed by Manchu officials and were able to work to their full potential. It was during this period that President Lincoln freed the slaves. America, the Chinese felt, was indeed a great country worthy of their loyalty. Democracy was an idea that they felt comfortable with. Perhaps they could not vote now, but soon, in the not-too-distant future, the ideas the Lincoln expressed—a nation of the people, by the people and for the people—would apply to them also.

From 1850 to 1870, California was an exceptional place. In the mountains there was gold; in the valleys, a bountiful agricultural wonderland was being born. The magnificent Pacific seacoast held the abundant treasures of a virtually untapped source of wealth. The riches produced by the gold, agricultural and sea products were bringing forth a new society.

Not only was there physical wealth, but there was also individual freedom. The issue of whether California would enter the union as a "free" state or a "slave" state had been newly decided. California would be free.

With an abundance of natural resources to develop, the growth of its cities financed by the seemingly unlimited supply of gold and a strong economy where everyone who wanted to work had a job, California for those brief twenty years was a special place. That sense of "specialness" was further accentuated by the fact that everyone who immigrated to California during those years had to work hard to get here. Everyone shared a "pioneer" spirit and a common goal of building the foundations of what would later be known as the "Golden State."

During that golden age, California was more like an independent kingdom than part of the United States. Cut off from the other states by high mountains and the Great Plains, California was free to develop a new society. But that was soon to change. A wave of new immigrants would hit the state, bringing the ills of the old world. The idyllic lifestyle that the early Californians developed would soon disappear.

7. The Clash of Civilizations: The Triumph of Racism

Exclusion and Expulsion of Chinese Americans from the Greatest Democracy in the World

What changed everything was the Transcontinental Railroad. Completed in 1869, by the following year California was being flooded by immigrants, many just arrived from Europe. Instead of the pioneers of the earlier era that earned their way to California through a soul-testing journey of heroic proportions, now all it took was short train ride of less than a week from the urban centers of the east. California would never be the same again.

The myth of race relations in California has been that there was a unified "White" race that started the anti-Chinese movement. In fact, there have always been two European-American positions on the Chinese questions. One was the "pioneer" position, which generally favored Chinese immigration. In that earlier era, when California was still a small state, these pioneers had firsthand knowledge of how much the Chinese had contributed to building the state and developing its resources. Many have identified these pioneers as capitalist, but it included people from across the economic and social spectrums.

The anti-Chinese side was taken by primarily newly arrived immigrants from Ireland, led by Denis Kearney. At that time, there were two kinds of "Whites": the lower-class Whites that Kearney represented and the higher-class Whites represented by the pioneers.

The history of America is one of erasing class distinctions between the different classes of "Whites." This process is called the "melting pot." It was a revolutionary process that unleashed immense potential as old-world hatreds were set aside. But there was a cost. To become White, there had to be an antithesis of White, a non-White that would serve as a catalyst or scapegoat. On the East Coast the scapegoat was African Americans (see *How the Irish Became White*, Ignatiev, 1995). On the West Coast, they were the Chinese.

Playing the "race card" brilliantly, Kearney soon had the established pioneers on the run. Not only did he want the Chinese excluded from immigration into America, he also wanted them expelled back to China. Kearney organized boycotts against companies using Chinese labor (the union label) and started a campaign to stop the employment of Chinese. In the small towns of California, the anti-Chinese forces organized the "League of Caucasians" and the "Caucasian Order." Many small-town Chinatowns—like Chico, Redding, Williams, Wheatland and Truckee— were torched and Chinese workers killed.

Not only was force used against the Chinese, the Anti-Chinese Movement also used it against Chinese sympathizers. Soon many of them were intimidated into giving up their ideas and ideals about a free and equal society open to all.

The promise of America has always been of a country that held itself open to all. We were a "land of opportunity," and by working hard, everyone could attain the American Dream.

The Anti-Chinese Movement was a test of those ideals. The issue was monumental. Was America going to close its doors to an immigrant group based on race? Congress confronted this issue by debating the merits of an "exclusion law" that would prevent the Chinese from immigrating to this country.

In 1876, Congress held a hearing on this question. Convening a Joint Special Committee of Congress on Chinese Immigration, they called 129 witnesses to testify. The testimony required 1,200 pages to report:

> *An analysis of the witnesses by occupations shows to what extent Chinese immigration had become a question of class and politics. The pro-Chinese witnesses included all the clergymen, diplomats, manufacturers, and men connected with railroads, navigation and foreign trade. The anti-Chinese witnesses included nearly all the officials, journalists, and workingmen...*
>
> *It appears to be a fair inference from this alignment that the demand for restriction or prohibition came from the working class, through the officials dependent upon their votes and the newspapers that voiced their wishes; and that the pro-Chinese party consisted of the large employing class, the humanitarians, and of those who had been intimately associated with the Chinese either in China or in this country.*
>
> *—Coolidge, Chinese Immigration, 1909*

More than half of the witnesses that testified, testified in favor of the Chinese. Notwithstanding that fact, the majority report, written by three members, all of whom were on record as being against Chinese immigration, came to conclusions that ignored the evidence. Instead they only repeated the arguments of the most rabid racists that testified. Senator Morton, the chairman of the committee, who unfortunately died prior to the publication of the report, reached more reasoned conclusions, based on the facts that were elicited during the hearing. The conclusions of the Special Committee, Senator Morton and Professor Becker of the University of Virginia have been summarized by Coolidge and set out to the right.

The majority report of the Special Committee of Chinese Immigration was the beginning of the end of free immigration to America. In 1882, the United States passed the Chinese Exclusion Act. The beacon of hope that the United States represented to all nations of the world had been dimmed. The racists had won an important battle. It would take another 61 years before freedom would ring again for Chinese Americans.

8. "Fan Qing": The Cantonese and China's Revolution

Starting with its defeat in the Opium War, China entered a slow period of decline. China under Manchu rule was no longer able to defend itself. It had been attacked on numerous occasions by foreigners since 1842 and had been defeated every time. The French and British won the Arrow War in 1860. The Russians annexed parts of Xinjiang in the 1870s. The French again fought China in 1884 and won. Japan and Germany soon joined and won their own wars against China.

Not only was China unable to defend itself against foreigners, it also faced rebellion from internal forces. The most important one, the Taiping Rebellion, started in 1851 and would last over a decade and affect millions of lives. Its leader, Hong Xiuquan, was Cantonese. The Boxer Uprising, the Nian Rebellion and the Red Turban Rebellion also took place during this time and were further signs that the Mandate of Heaven would soon be passing from the Qing.

As the Qing Dynasty started to show its weakness, the political question of the time was reform or revolution. Was the imperial system so ineffectual that only a revolution could save China, or was there still hope for the reform of the imperial system under a constitutional monarchy like Britain?

Coming from the most advanced and progressive part of the country, the Cantonese would play a major role in this debate. Leading the Reform Movement were the Cantonese scholars Kang Youwei and Liang Qichao. (Kang was from a county near Sze Yup, and Liang was from a Sze Yup county.)

As a scholar that had passed the highest level of the imperial examinations, Kang was thoroughly familiar with Confucian thought. By interpreting the Confucian Classics in a novel way he made the argument that were Confucius alive, he would be in favor of reform.

Kang's reputation grew and soon he caught the attention of the Guangxu Emperor. The emperor supported the reforms advocated by Kang and signed edicts that mandated reform. The Empress Cixi, then officially in retirement, was very displeased with the "Hundred Days of Reform." Acting swiftly, she had six reformers executed, repealed the edicts that had been signed and imprisoned the emperor.

Kang and Liang were forced to flee China. They would continue working on their cause, first in Japan, then eventually coming to America to start the Chinese Empire Reform Party and the Imperial Reform Army.

To many Chinese, the failure of the Hundred Days of Reform meant that more drastic action was needed. Another Cantonese leader soon emerged, the revolutionary Sun Yat-sen. Sun took the position that reform would not work; the imperial system was simply too outmoded for the modern world. A revolution to establish a republic was needed. In 1894 he formed the "Revive China Society." In 1895, he led an uprising in Guangzhou that failed. The Manchus tried to arrest and execute him, but he escaped abroad. Like Kang and Liang, Sun soon found himself in America, looking for support for his revolutionary ideas.

During this time, other Cantonese would play important roles in China's modernization. Yung Wing was the first Chinese to graduate from a major American college when he finished at Yale in 1854. He would later organize a program to send Chinese students to the elite eastern colleges of America. Wu Tingfan, the first Chinese barrister of Hong Kong, served as minister of justice and foreign affairs and was briefly acting premier during the early years of the Chinese republic.

The Cantonese dream of 250 years, "Fan Qing" ("Overthrow the Qing"), was starting to be realized.

9. BECOMING AMERICAN: THE CHINESE EXPERIENCE

Laying the foundations of the mining, agricultural, fishing and railroad industries, then fighting the Anti-Chinese Movement and the Exclusion Act and at the same time building Chinatowns and helping with the revolution in China, left Chinese Americans little time to become Americans.

For European Americans, there was a clear "melting pot" roadmap to follow. But the melting pot was not available to non-Whites. Instead of a pathway, the Chinese faced a minefield of obstacles. The most fundamental step to becoming American, citizenship, was closed to them. The Chinese quickly realized they would have to create their own pathway.

The obstacles the Chinese faced would delay the start of an American-born Chinese generation until the turn of the 20th century. But by that time a new problem had emerged. With the passage to the Exclusion Law and an unspoken policy of expulsion, Chinese Americans became the only immigrant group to come to America and face a dwindling population. In 1890 there were 107,488 Chinese in America. By 1900 that had been reduced to 89,863. In 1910 only 71,531 remained and in 1920, 61,639.

The declining population had an enormous impact on the Chinese American community, not the least of which was the psychological one. Any Chinese American child growing up during that period knew that it was only a matter of time before there would be no more Chinese in America. It was hard to work toward a future when there was no future to work toward. The great meeting of East and West would have proven to be a failure.

Chinese American businessmen faced problems not encountered by their European American counterparts. Every immigrant group before and after the Chinese could count on their communities increasing in size. With a population boom, a businessman would see an increase in his market; equally important he would have a supply of labor as new immigrants got established here. Chinese American businessmen did not have these advantages.

Workers and professionals also faced obstacles. Chinese Americans were barred from joining labor unions. The racists created the "union label," which everyone knew meant "European American labor" had been used to make that product; thus products without the label were most likely made by Chinese Americans. Professionals were prevented from getting licenses by using the "eligible for citizenship" barrier. The courts had ruled that the Chinese were not eligible for citizenship.

As part of the policy of expelling Chinese Americans, laws were passed at the federal, state and local levels, directed against the Chinese immigrants. These laws, the most important one being Exclusion, meant that the Chinese were spending an inordinate amount in time in court.

It wasn't merely the time that was spent in court; the Chinese eventually won almost all the cases that discriminated against them. When the lawmakers passed the discriminatory laws, they knew that many of them would never pass constitutional muster. They passed them anyway because they also knew that the laws would keep the Chinese tied up in court for years. The enormous expense of attorney and court fees would drain the Chinese American community from being able to advance in American society. The discriminatory way in which immigration laws were enforced often meant that a Chinese American man would be financially exhausted for trying to immigrate his wife and children into this country. With all his funds gone, the American Dream of starting one's own business would be forever out of his reach.

Yet in spite of the obstacles, a Chinese American culture started to emerge. In business, they started herbalist shops, grocery stores, laundries and restaurants. When they lacked capital, they formed partnerships. When there was opportunity away from the established Chinatowns, they left town. Soon all the small towns of California had at least one Chinese restaurant.

In education, even though there were no jobs waiting for them when they graduated, they never lost faith. They studied math, science and business—majors that had objective standards, so they at least had some prospects of employment. Starting in the '30s they were able to find employment in government jobs. These were the least discriminatory because they were protected by the civil service system. It wasn't until after Second World War that private firms started to hire the Chinese.

In sports and in their social life, stopped from participating in the majority society, they set up their own teams and social activities. The Wah Sung baseball team was organized in Oakland and played semipro ball. Oakland also fielded a female baseball team called the Oakland Dragonettes. In football, the Northern California Football League started. And in basketball, a number of leagues were formed, both in the Bay Area and Los Angeles, to compete with one another.

Social life centered on college and high school campuses with dances and parties. Many larger events were sponsored during the Lunar New Year, where the whole community participated.

In the face of enormous obstacles, a vibrant Chinese America was being born.

10. Chinese Americans: The Battle to Defeat Imperialism Abroad and Racism and Home—Victories at Last

At the turn of the 20th century, China had been "carved up like a melon" into "spheres of influence" by England, France, Germany, Russia and Japan. Chinese reform and revolution leaders knew that the first priority for the Chinese people had to be the defeat of these imperialist powers. They looked to Chinese Americans, with their access to Western military technology, as a vanguard for the building of a modern Chinese armed force.

The Cantonese reformers, Kang Youwei and Liang Qichao, both came to America seeking the support of Chinese Americans. Kang founded the Baohuanghui or Chinese Empire Reform Association in 1899. He visited a score of American cities, at each one forming branches of the Baohuanghui. By the time Liang arrived in the United States in 1903, there were fifty local chapters. San Francisco was the national headquarters. Kang was chosen as president and Liang as vice-president. The Baohuanghui quickly developed into the most powerful Chinese political group in America.

In 1903, the Western Military Academy was formed by the Los Angeles branch of the Baohuanhui. It was commanded by General Homer Lea, a European American who volunteered his services. He was later appointed by Dr. Sun Yat-sen to be Commander in Chief of the Revolutionary Army in China. Lea recruited as his drill sergeant Captain Ansel O'Bannion, who was responsible for training the troops. The Academy's mission was to train the Chinese Imperial Reform Army to defeat the Manchu forces in China. The Academy headquarters was located at 416 Marchessault Steet in Los Angeles' Old Chinatown. They trained and held maneuvers in Eagle Rock, a section of Los Angeles near Pasadena.

Starting with Los Angeles, branches of the Western Military Academy were soon formed in more than 21 cities, including St. Louis, Chicago, New York, San Francisco and Fresno. Over one thousand young Chinese American men volunteered.

Dr. Sun Yat-sen was also active in seeking the assistance of Chinese Americans to help strengthen China. Among his recruits was Tom Gunn, a pioneer aviator, often called the "Wright of China," who was born in San Francisco's Chinatown in 1890. In 1910, Gunn represented China at the International Aviation Meet in Los Angeles. When the revolution broke in China, Dr. Sun Yat-sen invited Gunn to China to set up a national Chinese air force.

Dr. Sun Yat-sen had visited the Delta area in California on several occasions in the early part of the 20th century. He recruited a number of young Chinese men that later became active in the Kuomintang. Chancy Chew, of Courtland, was one of them. In the 1920s Chew became an agent for Sun in charge of buying aircraft and training pilots and mechanics to be part of a national air force in China. Chew acquired several planes that were surplus equipment left over from World War I and set aside the back section of a ranch in Courtland for a base camp. Chinese American volunteers from the delta, Portland, Seattle and Honolulu signed up as volunteers. After months of hard work, the pilots and mechanics had been trained. On the eve of the day when the planes were to be sent to China, a fire broke out in the barn where they were stored, and all the planes were destroyed. But all was not lost. Many of the volunteers later went to China on their own or joined the American armed forces to fight the Japanese.

Chinese Americans not only volunteered to help China directly, but they also joined the American armed forces to help win the war for democracy. During World War II, Chinese Americans enlisted in the armed forces at close to double the percentage rate of the population as a whole. Like many Americans they served in every branch of service in every theater of war including Europe, the South Pacific, the North Atlantic and the China Burma India Theater. Most of the Chinese American servicemen served in integrated units. But two units, the 14th Air Service Squadron and the 987th Signal Company of the 14th Air Force (the Flying Tigers), were all Chinese Americans and served in China.

When China and America became allies in World War II, a hundred-year dream of Chinese Americans came true. For years, the Chinese in America hoped that their ancestral homeland and their adopted home would unite in a common cause. When Japan attacked Pearl Harbor, the United States and China joined together to defeat fascism in Asia. This alliance set the stage to help battle racism against the Chinese in America.

In 1943, Madame Chiang Kai-shek, China's first lady, visited the United States to strengthen ties between the two wartime allies. She spoke to a joint session of Congress and met with President Roosevelt. She was greeted by thousands of Chinese Americans during her tour of America. Madame Chiang, as well as the Chinese American communities, received a very favorable press. For the first time, European Americans saw a new Chinese America. Instead of the stereotypes of gamblers and opium dens, pictures of Chinese Americans looking very much like European Americans were in the nation's newspapers and magazines. Several months after Madame

Chiang's visit to America, the Chinese Exclusion Act was repealed. For the first time in our nation's history, the Chinese could become citizens of the United States.

With the repeal of the Chinese Exclusion Act, the racists had been beaten. America's true destiny, a country open to everyone, had been reaffirmed.

BIBLIOGRAPHY

All of our sources of information to prepare this book are listed here by category. Some of the information was recorded during the research in 2008 for our *Marysville's Chinatown* book in Arcadia Publishing's Images of America series. We are sorry to say that some of the elders whom we interviewed have passed on. We felt very fortunate, however, that we were able to capture much of the information before it was lost. There is an old Chinese proverb: "When an elder passes on, a whole library disappears."

BOOKS

Ah Tye Fakas, Lani. *Bury My Bones in America.* Nevada City, CA: Carl Mautz Publishing, 1998.

Architectural Resources Group. *Bok Kai Temple: Historic Structure Report.* San Francisco, CA: self-published, 2002.

Buschmann, Clark A., Principal, Buschmann Communications. *Third City.* Marysville, CA: Yuba Art Council, 1991.

Chace, Paul. *The Bok Kai Festival of 1931 in Historic Marysville: Creating a California Community.* Yuba City, CA: River City Printing, 1994.

———. *Dancing with the Dragon.* N.p.: self-published, 1994.

———. *A History of Marysville's Bok Kai Temple.* N.p.: self-published, 2015.

Chang, Iris. *The Chinese in America.* London: Penguin Books, 2003.

Chen, Shehong. *Being Chinese, Becoming Chinese American*. Champaign: University of Illinois Press, 2002.

Chen, Yong. *Chinese San Francisco, 1850–1943*. Palo Alto, CA: Stanford University Press, 2000.

Chinese Historical Society of America. *Chinese America: History and Perspectives*. Brisbane, CA: Fong Brothers Printing, 1991.

Chinn, Thomas. *Three Generations of Chinese—East and West*. San Francisco, CA: Chinese Culture Foundation of San Francisco, 1973.

Coolidge, Mary R. *Chinese Immigration (1909)*. Reprint, New York: Arno Press, 1969.

Criddle, Ruth. *Katie Lim: The Lady, The Legend, The Legacy*. Marysville, CA: self-published, 2004.

Daniels, Roger. *Asian Americans: Chinese and Japanese in the United States since 1850*. Seattle: University of Washington Press, 1988.

Delamere, Henry. "Chinese Tongs in Northern California." Marysville, CA: Unpublished.

———. *A Sketch of Marysville's History: The Early Years*. Marysville, CA: Barris Printing, 2001.

Ellis, W.T. *Memories: My 72 Years in the Romantic County of Yuba, California*. Eugene: University of Oregon, John Henry Nash Print, 1939.

Fairbank, John King. *The United States and China*. Cambridge, MA: Harvard University Press, 1983.

Garavaglia Architecture Inc. *Marysville Historic Commercial District—Historic Structure Impact Report*. San Francisco, CA: self-published, 2013.

Gee, Erika G. *At America's Gates: Chinese Immigration during the Exclusion Era, 1882–1943*. Chapel Hill: University of North Carolina Press, 2003.

Gee, Sherman. *Legacy of the Lone Sentinel*. San Francisco, CA: Andrew Benzie Books, 2016.

Hoobler, Dorothy, and Thomas Hoobler. *The Chinese American Family Album*. New York: Oxford University Press, 1994.

Hopkins, Tammy, and Henry Delamere. *Marysville*. Images of America Series. Charleston, SC: Arcadia Publishing, 2007.

Hsu, Francis L.K. *The Chinese of the American Dream: The Chinese in the United States*. Belmont, CA: Wadsworth Publishing, 1971.

Hsu, Madeline Y. *Dreaming of Gold, Dreaming of Home*. Palo Alto, CA: Stanford University Press, 2000.

———. *The Good Immigrants*. Princeton, NJ: Princeton University Press, 2015.

Hunsicker, Kelley. *Chinese Immigrants in America.* Mankato, MN: Capstone Publishers, 2008.

Ibanez, Reuben, ed. *Historical Bok Kai Temple in Old Marysville, California.* N.p.: Rose Printing Company, 1967. Published by the *Appeal Democrat.*

Jones, Anita W. *Door to Festivals, Feasts, Fortunes.* Taipei, Taiwan: Mei Ya Publications Inc., 1971.

Kin, Wong. *International Chinese Business Directory of the World for the Year 1913.* San Francisco, CA: International Chinese Business Directory Company Inc., 1913.

Kinkead, Gwen. *Chinatown: A Portrait of a Closed Society.* New York: Harper Perennial, 1993.

Kwong, Peter, and Dusanka Miscevic. *Chinese America.* New York: New Press, 2005.

Latsch, Marie-Luise. *Chinese Traditional Festivals.* Beijing, China: New World Press, 1984.

Li, Dun J. *The Ageless Chinese, a History.* New York: Charles Scribner's Sons, 1978.

Mark, Emily. "Most Popular Gods & Goddesses of Ancient China." Ancient History Encyclopedia, 2016. https://www.ancient.eu/user/emily.mark49.

McDannold, Thomas A. *California's Chinese Heritage: A Legacy of Places.* Stockton, CA: Heritage West Books, 2000.

Meltzer, Milton. *The Chinese Americans.* New York: Thomas Y. Crowell, 1980.

Minnick, Sylvia Sun. *Samfow: The San Joaquin Chinese Legacy.* Fresno, CA: Panorama West Publishing, 1988.

New-York Historical Society. *Chinese American Exclusion/Inclusion.* New York: Antique Collectors' Club Limited, 2014.

Ngai, Mae N. *The Lucky Ones: One Family and the Extraordinary Invention of Chinese America.* Boston: Houghton Mifflin Harcourt, 2010.

Roberts, J.A.G. *A Concise History of China.* Cambridge, MA: Harvard University Press, 2002.

Sacramento Chinese Culture Foundation & Asian-American Studies, University of California–Davis. *150 Years of the Chinese Presence in California (1848–2001).* Sacramento, CA: Sun Printing, 2001.

Sheafer, Silvia Anne. "Chinese and the Gold Rush." *Historical California Journal Publications.* N.p., 2001.

Shufen, Li. *Legends of Ten Chinese Traditional Festivals.* Beijing, China: Dolphin Books, 1994.

Spence, Jonathan D. *The Search for Modern China*. New York: W.W. Norton & Company, 1999.

Sung, B.L. *Mountain of Gold*. London: Macmillan Company, 1967.

Tom, Brian, and Lawrence Tom. *Marysville's Chinatown*. Images of America Series. Charleston, SC: Arcadia Publishing, 2008.

Tom, Edward George, Sr. (Poy Yee Tom). "The Story of My Life." Unpublished, 1987.

Tom, Henry. *Tan Genealogy: Heritage and Lineage*. Frederick, MD: self-published, 2009.

Tom, Raymond, MD. *10,000 Mile & 100 Years Journey from Jishi Village to Gold Mountain*. N.p.: self-published, 2004.

Tsai, Shih-shan Henry. *China and the Overseas Chinese in the United States, 1868–1911*. Fayetteville: University of Arkansas Press, 1983.

———. *The Chinese Experience in America*. Bloomington: Indiana University Press, 1986.

Interviews

Cejner-Meyers, Sue. Interviewed by Lawrence Tom, 2019.

Chan, Bertha Waugh. Interviewed by Brenda Lee Wong, 1993.

Chan, Bertha Waugh. Interviewed by Lawrence Tom, various years.

Croft, Doreen Foo. Interviewed by Dan Barth, 2004.

Gee, Betty Tom. Interviewed by Lawrence Tom, 1989.

Gee, Herbert. Interviewed by authors, various years.

Hom, Leonard, PhD. Interviewed by Lawrence Tom, various years.

Hom, Stanley. Interviewed by authors, 2007.

Kim, Frank. Interviewed by Dan Barth, 2004.

Kim, Frank. Interviewed by Lawrence Tom, 2007.

Kim, Jack. Interviewed by authors, 2007.

Lim, Charles. Interviewed by Eric Vodden, 2000.

Lim, Gene Sing. Interviewed by Lawrence Tom, 2007.

Lum, May Tom. Interviewed by Lawrence Tom, 2006.

Mar, Connie Tom. Interviewed by Lawrence Tom various years

Ong, Bing. Interviewed by Lawrence Tom, 2000.

Tom, Arthur, Jr. Interviewed by authors, various years.

Tom, Brian. Interviewed by Leonard D. Chan, Asian American Curriculum Project Inc., 2007.

Tom, Gordon. Interviewed by authors, various years.
Tong, Mary Ong. Interviewed by Lawrence Tom, 2019.
Waugh, Joe, Sr. interviewed by Brenda Lee Wong, 1971.
Wing, David. Interviewed by authors, 2008.
Wing, Ella Kim. Interviewed by Lawrence Tom, 2000.

NEWSPAPERS

Marysville Appeal.
Marysville Appeal Democrat.
Marysville Evening Democrat.
Marysville Herald.
Marysville Territorial Dispatch.
Sacramento Bee.
Sacramento Union.
Yuba City Daily Independent-Herald.

ONLINE SERVICES

California Digital Newspaper Collection. cdnc.ucr.edu.
California Historical Society Collection, University of Southern California Digital Library.
Calisphere. calisphere.univerityofcalifornia.edu.
Library of Congress.
University of Washington Libraries Digital Collections.

LIBRARIES

California State Library, California History Room.
Sacramento County Library.
Sutter County Library.
Yuba County Library, California Room.

INDEX

ABOUT THE AUTHORS

LAWRENCE (LARRY) TOM was born and raised in Marysville. He is a graduate of California State University–Sacramento (CSUS). He studied in the management program at the University of California–Davis (UCD). He was the comptroller, a career executive appointee (CEA), with the State of California, Department of Transportation (also known as CALTRANS). He is the tour director for the Chinese American Museum of Northern California (CAMNC). He was born and raised in Marysville. His interest is to preserve the early history of the Chinese pioneers in the area before it is lost.

BRIAN TOM is the founder of the Asian American Studies (AAS) program at the University of California–Davis, one of the first such programs in the country (founded in June 1969). He is a graduate of University of California–Berkeley (BA) and University of California–Davis (JD). He was an administrative law judge with the State of California and practiced law in San Francisco for more than twenty-five years. He is the founder and director of the Chinese American Museum of Northern California (CAMNC).

About the Authors

In 2006, Lawrence and Brian started writing books on Chinatowns in the Sacramento region and had three books published by Arcadia Publishing in the Images of America series. This is their fourth book and the first for The History Press.